LISA VANDERPUMP

SIMPLY DIVINE

A Guide to Easy, Elegant *and* Affordable Entertaining

Photographs by Jason Varney

Running Press
PHILADELPHIA • LONDON

THIS BOOK
IS DEDICATED

my grandmother Nanny Kay...who has sadly passed
and is still so very missed—a woman who lived her life
with elegance, grace, kindness, and style,
and who encouraged me to be the best I can be.
You will forever be in my heart.

Published by Running Press,
A Member of the Perseus Books Group

Books published by Running Press are available at special
discounts for bulk purchases in the United States by corpo-
rations, institutions, and other organizations. For more
information, please contact the Special Markets Depart-
ment at the Perseus Books Group, 2300 Chestnut Street,
Suite 200, Philadelphia, PA 19103, or call (800) 810-4145,
ext. 5000, or e-mail special.markets@perseusbooks.com.

ISBN 978-0-7624-4451-9

Library of Congress Control Number: 2011937765

E-book ISBN 978-0-7624-4522-6

9 8 7 6 5 4 3 2 1
Digit on the right indicates the number of this printing

Cover and interior design by Frances J. Soo Ping Chow
Edited by Jennifer Kasius
Food preparation by Carrie Purcell
Typography: Piel Script, Requiem, and Whitney

Running Press Book Publishers
2300 Chestnut Street
Philadelphia, PA 19103-4371

Visit us on the web!
www.runningpress.com

CONTENTS

Introduction

AT YOUR SERVICE

INCE I OPENED my life to the cameras for *The Real Housewives of Beverly Hills*, certain truths about me are now well-known: I was brought up in London. I married my husband of 29 years, Ken Todd, when I was 21. I am the mother of two beautiful children, Pandora, 25, and Max, 19. We have lived in the English countryside and the south of France, and now reside in Beverly Hills, California. We've owned 26 restaurants, bars, and clubs; our newest are Villa Blanca in Beverly Hills and SUR in West Hollywood. I have been writing for *Beverly Hills Lifestyle* magazine for the past three years (I have a deep passion for writing, as you will soon see!). And I am in love with a very sexy beast, my Gigolo, an adorable Pomeranian whom I call "Giggy" for short.

Of course, now everyone wants to know my *secrets*. Fair enough. I'll tell you. I'm afraid they're not very interesting. My life has been pretty conservative (rare for a *Housewife*, I know!). Even though I was a child actress, I've never had any of the scandalous problems that sometimes come of it—perhaps because I managed to stay away from the naughtiness, or perhaps because I just never got caught . . . I did have a fortunate upbringing, but when I left home, my parents didn't give me a penny. I worked two jobs to support myself.

So, what are my secrets? How did I do it—get from there to here? By taking risks, staying focused, never giving up, and working my rear off! I have always been a working mum, and my business is a very needy baby—open 16 hours a day! Aside from the restaurants, I also write and work on my skin care line, Epione. I'm a workaholic. I love working. And to me, if you're passionate about it, it's not really work. One of my mottos is: "Find something you love to do, and then you'll never have to work a day in your life."

8

When I got married, I taught myself to cook and found that I had a feeling for food. Ken and I have made food—the selection, preparation, and serving of it—our life's passion. And I'm delighted to share that passion with you.

But first, back to my secrets. How do I keep it all together? (And thank you for saying that, Darling, but it's all smoke and mirrors. More on that later . . .) Sorry, it's *not* plastic surgery (unusual for Beverly Hills, I know!). I get up early and get my arse on the treadmill every single day. This kind of work I really *don't* love. Would I let you get up there for me if I could? You bet I would! But it has to be done if one is to stay healthy, and being healthy is very important to me. Do I hate that in LA I'm surrounded by 6-foot-tall Amazonian supermodels? Of course. Do I hate that I have to back out of the bedroom so my husband can't see the dimples in my butt? Yes I do. When I see him reach for his glasses, I think, "Oh, thank goodness, his eyes are going just as I am starting to fall apart!" I try to concentrate on my positive physical attributes—which are slowly diminishing even as you are reading this. But let's not focus on that now . . .

Make yourself indispensable
to your loved ones. —*Lisa Vanderpump*

I will tell you my biggest secret of all—the one I'm asked to divulge more than any other. How have I stayed happily married for so, so long? It did help that I married my best friend, someone who makes me laugh, and "got" me from the word go. But how did I keep him—especially with all those supermodels sauntering into our restaurants? The same way I have kept my children close to me. It works for boyfriends, girlfriends, even my beloved furry friends. The trick? MAKE YOURSELF INDISPENSABLE TO YOUR LOVED ONES. Make them believe they cannot live without you, and they won't want to.

I've always thought it sad when I've heard people complain about taking care of their husband or children. It's an honor to be a caretaker—especially in the kitchen. I've never

found cooking to be a chore. It's a gift you give the people you love. I think it's one of the sexiest things you can do. (You didn't know you just bought a sex book, did you? But you did! A sexy, sumptuous book about food, friends, and family!) And as **I am always on the go rushing from here to there, when I do stop and spend time in the kitchen I find it's quite therapeutic. Making fresh food and serving it to your loved ones is good for the soul.**

And it doesn't take loads of money, I promise you. When our kids were small, Ken and I struggled, just like everyone else. The restaurant business is tough—especially in a difficult economy! But we've always had a great passion for life. And passion can override anything, even an empty bank account!

Beautiful things don't have to be expensive. In fact, I think the prettiest things are not: a single rose bud, a simple glass vase, a small, silver-colored tray with a vintage tea cup on it. The tray doesn't have to be real silver (that tarnishes anyway). I find the most delightful serving pieces at flea markets. Think outside the box and use what you already have to decorate your table: a strand of pearls, picture frames, a collection of votives . . .

I'm going to teach you how anyone from anywhere with any budget can make the ordinary extraordinary. In all my years of entertaining, I've learned simple is better, and usually much more beautiful. That's really what life is all about, isn't it? The simple and the divine.

One of the simplest acts of love you can give is through service. I love serving people—I've been serving someone or other most of my life. When I was a struggling actress in London, I waited tables. When you're a wife and a mother, you're serving

FOR THE LOVE OF
Dog

Because of his small size, Giggy goes everywhere with me, but he's not the only canine love of my life. When my children moved out and left me with a big empty house, I had no choice but to fill it with furry creatures. Besides Giggy, we have three other dogs: Lollipop, Pikachu, and Buki. I adore them all. I'm mad for dogs. I actually knew I would marry Ken when he pulled the car over so I could hop out and pet a passing puppy. (I still do that!)

everyone all the time, aren't you? And in the restaurant business Ken and I are serving people every day.

I love to serve people in my house—to open my heart and home to them. In a restaurant, you have to get up and leave at the end of a meal, but at home you have the luxury of time with your loved ones. I will show you how to make the most of your time with smart preparation and easy entertaining tips, so you can actually enjoy your guests.

This is not a fussy book. It's elegant, yes, but as we all know, elegance is learned, and money can't buy you class (if you're tardy for the party, however, I cannot help you. Really, I don't think anyone can . . .). I think you can tell I don't take myself too seriously. (I tried really hard to take myself seriously, but no one else would, so I had to give it up.) This book reflects that. It reflects me. Instead of being rigidly organized by course or season, I put it together by mood. However you're feeling, whatever you want to celebrate, you'll find simple suggestions for a beautiful meal with mix-and-match menus.

As a restaurateur, I have many sophisticated menus and recipes. Many of those recipes have gone from my kitchen to my restaurants and now into this book. A few are contributed by my chef Francis Dimitrius. But I can honestly say they are pretty uncomplicated, and will win you results that will hopefully impress your family and friends.

So often I wish I had made bigger quantities as it really doesn't take much longer, and is always gobbled up the next day (this was especially true when the children lived at home). Almost all of the recipes in this book will keep really well for a few days—with the exceptions of a few salads, although their dressings will keep. (Many dishes taste even better a few days later, but make sure they are always well refrigerated.)

Many of my friends are intimidated by entertaining, dreading the thought of an audience witnessing their latest culinary disaster. But I tend to see the humor in most situations. If things go awry when you are entertaining—and trust me, I have had my share of catastrophes like a dish exploding with all my roast potatoes in it on Christmas Day—take a second, take a step back, and just laugh. If you laugh at yourself, your friends will laugh with you, too.

And if something goes wrong, keep it all in perspective. A war wasn't lost, a heart wasn't broken . . . I take serious things seriously. A broken plate or a belated party guest are not serious things in my book.

And seeing as how this is my actual book, I will make the rules, and break them as I see fit. I'm delighted to invite you into my world of simply divine entertaining. Welcome!

— *Lisa Vanderpump*

13

CHAPTER

{ I }

Preparation

BEFORE WE GET into my true passion—presentation—I want to take a moment to prepare you. As you've heard, an ounce of prevention is worth a pound of cure. The more prepared you are for entertaining, the less stressful it will be, and the less likely something is to go amiss.

- - - - - - - PLAN A GOOD MENU -

Write it all down before you commit to anything to make sure that you've got a balanced menu, that you can in fact obtain all of the ingredients you need, and that it suits your time requirements. If you plan it all out before you start running around cooking, you can ensure that each course flows into the next and your food choices complement one another.

And never, ever serve messy food at a party: no corn on the cob, artichokes, or crab you must crack out of its shell.

- - - - - - - PRE-MAKE THE FOOD -

After you've selected your menu, look at your time schedule and decide when you might make the dishes. Make anything you can ahead of time so that on the day of your gathering, you're only heating things up. When you garnish them with beautiful, fresh items just before serving, no one will ever be the wiser. If you are serving three courses, plan to make at least one course the day ahead.

- - - - - - - PRE-PARE THE GARNISHES -

Gather and prep all your garnishes the day before (although you should wait to fan the strawberries or spiral the cucumber until just before serving so the garnish is fresh). Decide how you are going to top your food and decorate the plates, and get those items ready. This will save you time the day of, and ensure you have enough of everything. I often sketch

16

little drawings of the courses so I can visualize how they might look. (I'll give you my restaurant secrets to the art of "plating" in the next chapter.)

------- PRE-PREP YOUR INGREDIENTS -------------------------------------

Do most of your prep work the day before, if that's at all possible. Getting all your measuring and peeling and chopping and mincing done will save you loads of time the next day.

------- PRE-SET THE TABLE -------------------------------------

I always set the table the day before, and make sure I have everything on the table that I'll need, including non-refrigerated condiments (just make sure to cover them with plastic wrap!).

PROPER TABLE SETTING

AFTER WE WERE married a few years, Ken and I were lucky enough to know a butler who was engaged in royal service, so I have it on good authority how to set a proper table. We don't pay so much attention to details like this anymore in everyday life, but whenever you have anyone into your home, I think you should set the table correctly. The precision and order and beauty of it add so much to the meal. You've worked your tail off preparing a lovely dinner; it would be a shame to just slop it on the table with forks and knives scattered everywhere. By setting a formal table, you're letting your guests know from the moment they enter the room how much care and thought you've given to your gathering.

Here is a helpful guide to setting a formal table. Set your dinner plates down first so you can build the setting around them. Think of the dinner plate as the center of a clock.

TABLE SETTING

RED WINE

WATER

WHITE WINE

SOUP SPOON

SALAD KNIFE

DINNER KNIFE

DESSERT SPOON

DESSERT FORK

DINNER PLATE

APPETIZER PLATE

BREAD PLATE

DINNER FORK

SALAD FORK

Dinner Plate

Place it in the center of the seating, 2 inches from the edge of the table. Try to space the plates 2 feet apart. Appetizer plates are set on the dinner plate and then removed. The bread plates are set at 10 o'clock.

Silverware

For ordering, remember you eat "from the outside in." You should set up the knives and forks so that the ones on the outside are used first. Forks on the left at 9 o'clock; knives and spoons on the right at 3 o'clock. Nearest the plate should be the dinner fork and dinner knife. Next up are the salad fork and salad knife. A soup spoon may be placed to the right of the salad knife. A dessert fork goes horizontally above the dinner plate at 12 o'clock, tines facing the knives. A dessert spoon goes horizontally above the dessert fork, bowl facing the forks. A bread knife rests horizontally across the bread plate. All knife blades should be turned towards the plate.

Glasses

Water glasses are set at 1 o'clock. Red wine glass to the right of it; white wine glass to the left of it.

FORWARD MEN

Don't get upset or offended if under the tablecloth a man, other than the one you came with, puts his hand on your knee. You don't need to upset the party to expose him. Just pick up his hand, put it on the table in plain sight, give it a firm pat, and you'll get your message across. If he keeps it up, then you have my permission to give him a little pinch on the inside of the thigh.

Napkins & Napkin Rings

I use linen napkins held in napkin rings that I set across the dinner plate. I've collected beautiful napkin rings over the years, but you can make them quite easily yourself. Simply buy a reel of wired ribbon, tie it into a bow, and stick a fresh rose or sprig of flowers in it.

PLACE CARDS

WHILE SOME PEOPLE do buffets and do them well, I hate them. It's a personal thing, but I just find the buffet line so uncomfortable: Where do you sit? Do you heap your plate

all at once to avoid the embarrassment of returning trips? Do you use multiple plates for cold and hot, or just let things run all over each other? For a formal gathering, I would never, ever do a buffet.

I am a firm believer in assigned seating to avoid any awkwardness or confusion for your guests. As the hostess, you should be sensitive to who might like to sit next to whom (and who needs to be far, far away from the crazy redhead with the electronic cigarettes).

Of course, this means you must have place cards, and for me that's half the fun of entertaining. There are so many creative ways to do place cards, and people love to see their name written out. I always handwrite the place cards; never do it on the computer, it's too impersonal.

You can use a folded card stock, but here are a few of my more creative favorites:

Tiny Frames

Use small photo frames for holding the name cards. I have an assortment of little silver frames just for this purpose. You can find them very cheaply in any number of stores.

Parties are to be enjoyed! Remember the mantra: Keep calm and carry on. —*Lisa Vanderpump*

Photo Cards

Either tucked into a frame or glued to a card, I like to use photos of my guests, smiling and happy ones, of course, sometimes from the last time we were together. Everyone loves to see which picture I've chosen, and it always gets the conversation going. Don't forget to make one for yourself; mine has a picture of my darling Giggy and me.

Ornament Balls

Whether it's Christmastime or not, you can use colored glass balls as place cards. (Bright pink ones look fabulous!) Use a paint marker to write out each guest's name.

Name Tags

Handwrite the names on little strips of paper, punch a hole through them, and attach them to the napkin ring, or a sprig of flowers or herbs placed on the plate, like a little name tag on a present. It's a lovely gesture since the meal is your gift to them.

Personalized Napkin Ribbon

Get a wide, dark ribbon, like a lovely crimson or whatever matches your table color palette, and tie it around the napkins in a large bow or loose knot. Handwrite each guest's name on the end of the ribbon. Finish it off with a little spray glue and glitter.

Food Holders

Depending upon the season, place a small pumpkin, squash, or apple at each seat. Cut a slit into the top and slip in the place card.

-------- PLAN TO NOT GET UP ---

Have everything on the table so you don't have to get up once you are seated—even a water jug with slices of lemons or limes for drink refills. If you can, get someone who's not eating to serve the courses for you so you're not constantly hopping up and down, dashing back and forth between the dining room and the kitchen. If your children are older, you can certainly use them and their friends, or local high school students, or of course you could hire someone. Letting someone else do the serving, even though you've cooked the food yourself, will add to your ability to enjoy the evening enormously.

While you want enough room at the table, when you're having a party, there's nothing worse than a room that's too big. It's always better to choose a smaller room and to have people squished together and cozy. A party scattered all over the house is no good; never do that. Parties don't work well when they're fragmented. Force people together into a smaller, single space and the atmosphere will be so much better.

SERVING PIECES

I BUILT MY COLLECTION up over many years. I always kept an eye out for classic, neutral pieces that would carry me through the different fads and fashions. Collect as many different shapes and sizes of white, silver, or clear pieces as you can. It doesn't have to be real china, silver, or crystal. If you keep your pieces polished and dusted, they will look just as lovely.

Don't worry about everything matching. It's actually better if everything is mismatched, as long as each piece is a neutral color. In English hotels, very often the silverware is mismatched and it looks wonderful. Flea markets are especially good for finding interesting serving pieces, as are online auction sites and estate sales. Who knows, you just might find a treasure!

A few of the more unique serving pieces I use again and again when entertaining are:

Soup Tureen with Ladle

I have two: a large silver and a white one, both neutral colors so they match any theme. As you will see with my homemade soup recipes, I like to serve soup at the table. It's a comforting and elegant touch.

Cake Stand

If you have a great cake stand, it will last you through years of entertaining. It literally elevates your dessert. I have quite a few; it's something I can't seem to stop collecting (what does that say about my love of cake?).

Tiered Dessert Stand

A nice 3-tiered dessert stand set to the side, decorated with rose petals and fresh fruit, makes a statement before your party's even begun.

Oversized Platters

Large platters are hard to find, but they make an enormous impact when you're serving guests. I'll show you why in Chapter 8, but suffice it to say, scoop them up whenever you see one for purchase.

HOSTESS DUTIES

ONCE YOUR PARTY is all planned out, you've got to prepare yourself! The most important thing you must do is not stress too much. Parties are to be enjoyed! Remember the mantra: Keep calm and carry on. If I may, a few tips to help you keep a clear head:

Hostess Gifts

If one of your guests brings you a gift, open it immediately in front of them so they may see your appreciation. No matter what it is, tell them how very much you love it. Even if you think it's hideous—and believe me, just because I like pink doesn't mean I like *everything* pink!—or it secretly hurts your feelings, as in a joke gone wrong, don't let on. Assume that anyone bearing a gift has good intentions and only means the best for you.

If someone brings you flowers, put them in water immediately; don't let them wilt off to the side. Put them in a pretty vase and place them where everyone can enjoy them.

You do not have to send a thank you note for hostess gifts; your guests are thanking you for inviting them.

Room for Coats

Always have a place for coats, straight away, even if it's just a little room. You don't want coats hanging all over your sofa's arms.

Catastrophe

If anyone ever smashes anything, even an heirloom, immediately say: "It doesn't matter. It's absolutely not important. I didn't like it anyway." If they spill a drink, even if you want to strangle them, which, trust me I've wanted to, tell them it's no big deal. Just blot it up, cover it with a clean napkin, and deal with it the next day. There's absolutely no upside to making anyone feel worse than they already do. You'll do better to be gracious, especially since your mood will dictate the mood of the entire party.

Conversation Killers

As the hostess, it is your duty to keep the conversation moving in the right direction. If people are itching for a fight, let them do it at their own party! Conversations everyone should steer clear of include politics, religion, and childrearing. (Isn't it interesting that often the best parents are the ones without children!) I adore lively conversations, don't get me wrong, but if you think you can change someone's views at a dinner party, you need your head examined!

Starting Time

Always arrange the starting time of your party to be 45 minutes before you plan on sitting down to eat. That will give everyone plenty of time to arrive, get drinks, and mingle. If I start the party at 7 p.m., I will begin seating everyone at 7:45 p.m. Since you've already built in time, there is no need to wait for anyone arriving later than that. I don't wait, I just serve the food, and usually those belated guests get the message and try harder to be on time for the next dinner party.

Music

You should always play music at your parties. It will not only help create the mood you're trying to set, and soothe any "savage beasts" in the room, but it is also a very important aural cue. When you are ready for the party to end, simply shut off the music. People will get the message. For those who don't, an "oh dear, everyone else has left," or "you must be exhausted" should do the trick.

Choose music that you love, but that also matches the theme of your party. Soft music is better suited for times when you wish to be able to speak to your guests; dance music should be reserved for times when you're actually dancing. Light classical and jazz are wonderful choices to accompany a serious dinner.

I have an extensive collection of songs I use in our restaurants and for my personal entertaining. Here's a small sampling—it's a little mix of everything from Gipsy Kings to the First Lady of France, that will set a pitch-perfect mood for any party.

"ANGELS" by Robbie Williams; "L'EXCESSIVE" by Carla Bruni; "BELLA LUNA" by Jason Mraz; "DESIRE" by Deepak Chopra featuring Demi Moore; "NO ORDINARY LOVE" by Sherrie Lea; "ARIA ON AIR" by Malcolm McLaren; "FLY ME TO THE MOON" by Frank Sinatra; "TOI JAMAIS" by Catherine Deneuve; "IF YOU DON'T KNOW ME BY NOW" by Seal; "DON'T KNOW WHY" by Norah Jones; "DESERT ROSE" by Sting; "CAN'T TAKE MY EYES OFF YOU" by Muse; "TO LOVE SOMEBODY" by Nina Simone; "WAITING IN VAIN" by Bob Marley; "TIME OF OUR LIVES" by Paul van Dyk; "TRISTA PENA" by Gipsy Kings; "UN LUGAR" by Federico Aubele; "NO WOMAN NO CRY" by Jonathan Butler; "EVERYTHING" by Michael Bublé

CHAPTER

{ 2 }

Presentation

HIS IS GOING to be my favorite chapter, I can tell already, because to me, presentation is everything! I love putting things together. I've been the sole interior designer for all of our clubs and restaurants, as well as each one of our houses. Ken and I have moved house at least a dozen times in our marriage, and I think we will continue to do so. I just love the challenge of creating a new look.

I think I've been successful so far. I've been asked many times to design interior spaces for others. A woman came into Villa Blanca three times to ask if I would please help her. "Just consult on the design!" she said. I finally agreed, and met her at her house. As we walked around, my mind was filling with ideas, and I felt quite excited at the prospect of helping her. She announced she had already finished one room, the kitchen, and thought it was just perfect. When she opened the kitchen door, my chin hit the floor. It was the complete antithesis of anything that I would ever create. I knew then and there that I don't have the temperament to be a designer for anyone else.

Even if you've only just designed in your own home, you can rest confidently on your own skills. I think your house is the most important thing you can decorate. My house is my sanctuary. I am lucky enough to have a husband that likes my taste even to the point of him sleeping in a pink master bedroom!

Finances of course will dictate how lavishly you may decorate, but my style has always been sexy, warm, and attainable above all. I love to mix things up: items you collect on your

MY JEWEL

One of my favorite places we ever owned was a club called Jewel. It was huge, and right in the middle of Piccadilly Circus in the very center of London. It contained four themed bars whose décor was inspired by Baz Lurhmann's *Moulin Rouge.* It was dripping with rich Bordeaux colors and furnishings, with candles everywhere and absolutely breathtaking chandeliers dancing with jewels. Our opening night was a private party for the fortieth birthday of David Furnish, Elton John's husband. David and Victoria Beckham were frequent guests. And my lips shall stay sealed at that.

travels mixed with finds from the local flea market. I will sometimes buy a special piece and hold onto it until I find a suitable place or project for it.

MY S&M: SMOKE AND MIRRORS

While I have traveled the world and made my living decorating beautiful spaces, it's not entirely what it seems. My life is all smoke and mirrors: On the outside it looks good, but you have no idea what's underneath! As long as you put your best foot forward, there's no reason anyone need know you're faking it beneath the shine and shimmer!

Remember that with a few dramatic statements and lovely details you can hide almost anything. No one can see your old table when it's covered by a luscious tablecloth. Did the top of your dessert not come out perfectly? Dust it with some powdered sugar and

VILLA FLEURIE

The name of my house in Beverly Hills is Villa Fleurie. Do you not name your houses in America? We all do in Britain. It has nothing to do with size or grandeur; it's just a delightful custom. Anyone can name their house—you just pick a name when you move in. Some people choose to name their house for an ancestor; some for what the house used to be; but it can be whatever you like. Some of my previous houses: Shipton Sollars Manor, Villa Aujourdhui, and La Fleur Blanche. I love the idea because it adds an extra, more personal dimension to entertaining and making memories. Most people get a little sign made up with their house name and hang it by the front door, but you can do so much more. You can have napkin rings engraved with the name of your house; add it to guest towels, letterhead . . . Let's get this started in America, shall we? I propose you name your house right now, and then throw a party to celebrate it!

My Morning S&M

Iam a firm believer in getting yourself ready in the morning top to toe, hair washed, make-up on, before you leave the house. Yes, I'll admit when the children were small I did sometimes drive them to school in my pajamas. And it was Sod's Law (Murphy's Law, I believe you call it) that every time I tried to escape unnoticed, I would run into the last person on this planet that I wanted to see me looking a disheveled mess!

I believe if you take care of yourself first in the morning, your frame of mind is different and you will be prepared for all eventualities. I, at least, now that my children are grown, will try to never give it up again. I think I will color my hair until they carry me off in a box!

pop on a few fresh flowers. (A dusting of powdered sugar over rose petals looks like freshly fallen snow.) I use double-sided tape to stick down small vases on trays. I use berries and cut roses and flower petals to distract from many things. If you look under the covers at my dessert table—plates of goodies all set at different heights—you'll find stacks of books piled up and covered with fabric. A beautiful presentation can turn even the simplest display into a visual feast.

Trays

Trays are a wonderful, very simple way to keep your guests focused on beautiful things. A basic tray, even a glass one, with a little flower arrangement in the middle makes any dessert, tea, or coffee seem that much more posh. There is nothing easier for dessert than arranging fancy chocolates or beautiful mints in a crystal candy dish carried in on a silver tray with little flowers scattered around. It takes absolutely no time, costs next to nothing, and makes a huge impact.

I also use little silver trays on the table for serving dry condiments. It's easier to pass them around the table, and gives them a presence.

Lighting

Good lighting is essential to a beautiful presentation. It can make or break the mood of your party. Bad lighting can ruin everything. It's why you go into the dressing room to buy a swimsuit and come out with a muumuu. They shine such a harsh light on every imperfection!

Always go for soft lighting. Use dimmers if you can. Natural light is wonderful. And nothing is better than candles, and lots of them—tall ones, short ones, votives hidden everywhere. Instant magic.

Dressing up a Store-Bought Dessert

One of my greatest tricks is to dress up a store-bought dessert. You may have seen me doing this when Kyle and her daughter Portia were in my kitchen on one of the *Real Housewives* episodes. I bought a lovely cake covered with a simple chocolate ganache, very plain looking. I put it on a cake stand, and pressed fresh flowers into it: a large arrangement of pink roses on top and smaller flowers around the sides. There is nothing prettier, and it takes no time at all. (Just make sure your guests don't mistakenly eat any blooms if you're not using edible flowers!)

Color

If there's one color I like as much as pink, it's white. It's a beautiful blank canvas that allows other colors to pop. My house is almost entirely white because it gives me the freedom to change accessories and flowers without redecorating!

No matter what the occasion or celebration, you can always start with white as your backdrop. A white tablecloth and white plates will allow the food to pop. You can then choose an accent color or two, and accessorize with napkins, plate chargers, table runners, centerpieces, and flowers.

Black is another wonderful neutral color that creates a striking palette with other accent colors—and it instantly adds masculinity.

ARRANGING FLOWERS

I like to use natural décor wherever I can, and there's nothing more natural, or beautiful, than fresh flowers. Flowers to me are an essential part of my existence, an integral part of the harmony I require to live a well-balanced life. The perfume they emit can transform a room. They are juicy, succulent pieces of living art. They are the centerpiece of any party I have.

I have a passion for flower arranging. I'm most definitely an amateur, but what I lack in experience, I make up for with enthusiasm!

At both Villa Blanca and SUR, huge flower arrangements are an important part of the ambiance and pride of place. I buy, choose, and arrange the towering arrangements for each restaurant myself

> ### PINKY
>
> Although that guy Ken who lives with us calls her "Lisa," Mistress is known to most everyone else as "Pinky." Judging from the number of pink shoes and purses in her closet (I've been warned not to chew on the Louboutins), I'd say it's because she loves the color pink. Her friend Martin, the one who went on a blind date with Kim Richards on the show, gave her the name years ago. I'd be jealous that he's known her longer, but I know she loves me more. Tum ti tum tum. —*Giggy*

every week. It would be ridiculously expensive to go to a florist with the amount of flowers we need for restaurants, so a trip to the wholesale flower mart is mandatory. I would have to pay a florist thousands of dollars a month; I do it myself for $150 (look at the Villa Blanca Web site and you'll see how gigantic my arrangements are!). Most larger cities have a wholesale mart—I highly recommend you find yours and get your flowers from there. They are very affordable and a delightful place to visit. The flower market in Los Angeles

is a lively scene in the heart of the city, full of a mesmerizing hustle and bustle you don't often see. And of course if you cut flowers from your own garden, you will save a fortune!

Choosing Flowers

Try to select long-living flowers to make your arrangements last.

Live longest: Orchids, gladiolas, carnations, mums, Peruvian lilies, delphiniums

Live long: Roses, lilies, peonies, sunflowers

Short lived: Irises, Gerbera daisies, tulips, daffodils, lilac

Conditioning Flowers

If you "condition" your cut flowers before you arrange them, they can last up to twice as long. Snip an inch off the bottom of their stems with a slanted cut, and set them carefully in a large plastic bucket filled just one-third with warm water mixed with flower preservative. Don't crowd them, and don't allow any foliage to rest in the water. Set the bucket in a cool, dark place for at least four hours, preferably overnight. This will give them a chance to fill entirely with water, crisping up the blooms.

While they look hardy, flowers with woody stems such as hydrangeas and lilacs have the hardest time taking in water because they seal up at the bottom. Using the tip of your scissors, split their stems for two inches from the bottom to help them stay hydrated.

Flower Preservatives

Bacteria in the water hastens the wilting of your flowers. Make sure you use a clean vase, and wash the stems before submerging them to remove any bacteria. Flower preservatives, found at almost any place that sells flowers, contain bacteria-killing chemicals, an acidifier to help the plant drink, and sugar to feed it. Add it to the water before placing the flowers in the vase. You can also make your own by adding a capful of household bleach, a teaspoon of sugar, and a teaspoon of lemon juice to your water. And remove dead flowers from the bunch immediately, as they emit a gas that causes their neighbors to wilt.

If you use flower preservatives, you only need to change the water in the vase twice a week. If you don't, you must change it daily.

There's nothing more natural, or beautiful, than fresh flowers. They are juicy, succulent pieces of living art.—*Lisa Vanderpump*

Villa Blanca

I put my love of white to the test when designing Villa Blanca. As you can imagine from its name, it's almost entirely white—a brave choice in a restaurant where people are eating! Opening a restaurant at all in a recession is a bold move; Ken and I were met with a lot of disbelief when we started. But we believed that if the restaurant was visually stunning as well as affordable, and fulfilled a niche no one else had, it could be successful.

I wanted Villa Blanca to be more than just a restaurant; I see it as a whole lifestyle. My vision was to create a place that had flavors from England, France, and even Asia, with eclectic décor but the relaxed feel of a European café. I designed the entire space, top to bottom, new walls to windows, in just six weeks. I lined the restaurant with glass doors to give it an indoor/outdoor airy feel. White leather banquets with linen pillows and padded chairs encourage you to sit back and relax. It's friendly and informal, while also being elegant and someplace you never really want to leave—which is really good since Ken, Giggy, and I practically live there!

Building Arrangements

Many people are intimidated by arranging their own flowers, but it's really simple, I promise you. You needn't have studied how to do it and there are no rules. Just put your heart into it!

The secret is to start with filler. I use lots and lots of green fillers and baby's breath. Filler will make your arrangement twice as big, separate the different flowers beautifully, and is wonderfully inexpensive. Fill your vase with your background filler first, and then strategically place the more expensive flowers. Another simple way to create a professional-looking arrangement is to choose all different flowers the same shade of color.

I always arrange my flowers the day before a party. Keep in mind where your guests will be sitting. You want them to see the flowers, but also each other! Many times I've created a gorgeous arrangement for dinner only to realize that night that my guests had to talk through a forest. To remedy this, I always make my arrangements either very high, on narrow stands, or very low. I also like to put flower arrangements at both ends of the table and seat everyone in between them.

The Secret to Beautiful Low Arrangements

The key to gorgeous, low-lying arrangements that you can easily speak over—gush over, really—is floral foam. You can get blocks of floral foam at your local craft store, florist, or online. Get a waterproof tray—even a serving dish will do—and cut the foam to fit inside it. Tape the foam down with floral tape in a cross pattern over the top and sides to help you evenly distribute your blooms. Trim the corners off, and stick a small knife into the top of the brick in several places, twisting it a bit to get a small "x" shape to allow the water to seep in and not just run off. Slowly add water to the foam, and allow it to soak for 10 minutes before you start filling it with flowers.

Cut the flower stems at an angle so they will slide in easily. Start by inserting long stems next to the tape on all four sides. Continue adding flowers to the bottom and sides to just brush the table top but cover the tray. Add the same flowers to each opposite side for even coverage. Now press in your largest, most dramatic flowers to the top center. Add the rest of your flowers to the top sides. Finally use filler greens and baby's breath to fill in all the gaps.

You can make any number of arrangements, even line up trays and foam blocks to create a single row that spans the entire length of the table.

The Secret to Beautiful High Arrangements

The key to lovely tall arrangements is a funny little floral accessory called a pin frog. While floral foam only lasts for one arrangement, a pin frog is a permanent little helper. It's a heavy, flat-bottomed object made of metal with spiky points on top. You place it in the bottom of your vase and it helps the flowers stand up and separate from one another. You can find pin frogs for just a couple dollars at craft stores, floral supply stores, and online.

Vases

While solid or patterned vases are lovely, I prefer to use clear glass or crystal so that the flowers may be the focal point, and they will suit any occasion or theme. I often fill vases with cut lemons or limes or other natural items to complement my décor. Another trick I often use is to put a large piece of clear cellophane in the vase and sprinkle it with rose petals. When you fill the vase with water, you won't be able to see the cellophane, but the petals will seem to float suspended.

ARRANGING FOOD

Now that we've talked about how to decorate your space and arrange your flowers, let's focus on making the food beautiful!

-------- THE ART OF PLATING --

You don't have to go to culinary school to master the art of arranging food on the plate so it's a feast for the eyes as well as the mouth. Far too many people get intimidated when they see how chefs plate their creations, but with a few simple tips, it's really quite easy.

Use large plates. We've talked about this before, but it bears repeating: Larger plates are better for serving beautiful food. You don't want your food to look crowded; the negative space around each item gives the entire plate balance and energy.

Use white dishes. This allows the food to stand out and make a statement, rather than the little painted leaves or scallops on the plate. A neutral base also gives you the opportunity to pull a complementary color from your food into your table setting. For instance, a red tomato soup in a white bowl with a pinch of green parsley on top looks gorgeous when set on a green napkin that matches the parsley and complements the soup's color.

Use color groupings. Keep same-colored foods together—all the carrots in one pile rather than spread around the rim of the entire plate for example. But keep like color piles separate. If you're serving asparagus and green beans, separate them with red tomatoes or yellow corn.

Use complementary colors as garnishes. As mentioned with the soup, try and contrast the color of your food with differently colored garnishes. If the food on your plate is mostly green, don't add green parsley to the side. Instead, find a red or yellow, such as a teardrop tomato cut in half.

Use the middle of the plate. Start in the middle of the plate to set out your meal rather than spreading everything all over the place. This will give the plate a focal center and also keep servers' thumbs from accidentally slopping into someone's food!

Use height. Try and raise the food in the middle of the plate. The starch is usually good for this: Scoop rice into a tall mound, pile up the mashed potatoes . . . then lean your main meat against the mound to raise it up a bit.

Use hot or cold dishes. Hot food stays hot longer on a warm plate. You can warm dishes in the oven or microwave, provided they are safe for those uses, or simply run them under hot water for a few seconds. Cold dishes can be stored in the freezer or refrigerator for a short time.

Use edible garnishes. Parsley and mint are perfect garnishes and should be kept on hand at all times. Sliced citrus fruit is also a great accompaniment for almost anything. Small cherry, grape, or teardrop tomatoes—especially in the more unusual orange or yellows— are delightful. Just be sure to wash your garnishes so they may be eaten, and don't serve anything inedible. A bough of pine might look lovely on the table in December, but don't put anything on your guests' plates you don't want them to eat.

Use odd numbers. For some odd reason, our eyes appreciate looking at items that aren't counted evenly. Put five meatballs on the plate rather than six; three roasted potatoes rather than four.

Use sauces . . . sparingly. Rather than pooling sauce on a plate or covering your wonderful food with it, use just a hint on the plate and allow guests to help themselves to more in sauce bowls on the table. A single stripe of sauce on an empty part of the plate dripped off the end of a spoon is the safest bet. You can also get a plastic squeeze bottle to fill with sauce for more delicate lines, swirls, or dots. Green pesto sauce is a lovely garnish for savory dishes. And I adore chocolate sauce on anything sweet.

Use paper towels. These are invaluable for wiping away any drips or juices around the edges of your plates before you serve them.

Use deep breathing. You needn't stress yourself out about building the perfect plate. In fact, you can overdo it. Don't try and build the Eiffel Tower out of carrot sticks. A simple, neat, organized plate with a single, long sprig of cilantro or chive set across the top of everything is all you really need.

------- READY, STEADY, GO! ---

I've worked up an appetite with all this planning! Let's get into the kitchen, shall we, and start cooking up a feast!

47

NO PLASTIC BOTTLES ...
EVER!

If I have one steadfast rule it is this: Never put a big plastic bottle on the table. I don't care if it's summer, I do not want to see a big bottle of ketchup or horseradish or anything with a giant label anywhere near my food . . . ever! To me it's like going out without make-up on, an almost unforgivable offense. Some things need to be disguised, and plastic bottles are one of them. I always put my ketchup, mustard, horseradish, cheese, and other condiments in little serving bowls so marketing slogans don't scream over and ruin the beautiful ambience I worked so hard to create.

CHAPTER

{3}

HETHER YOU HAVE a sexy beast like Giggy (or Ken), or you just want to snuggle in with your children, Cozy Days are divine. The season doesn't matter. Of course snowy winter days beg for a cozy set-up, but so can a spring shower or even just the dark of night. What is important is that the atmosphere is inviting, the food comforting, and your guests covered with the warmth of your love.

A BUSY COOK'S BEST FRIEND: PRE-MADE BROTH

For years I sweated over the stove, wrestling chicken carcasses to make my own stock. And then I discovered the miracle of modern, organic, low-sodium prepackaged chicken broth. Whole Foods' powdered vegetarian "chicken" broth is amazing. It will change your life! But you don't have to use powdered (although I swear by it). You can use boxed, frozen, or canned as well. I've also heard good things about Trader Joe's and Imagine brands. Just be sure to choose an organic, reduced-sodium option. I wish someone had told me years ago!

. . .

STOCK VS. BROTH

You might have heard differently, but I have it on very good authority that there is no difference between stock and broth (I use the word "stock" in most of these recipes). There might have been at one time a difference in how they were each prepared, but today the words are used interchangeably on labels, mostly for marketing as some believe "stock" sounds more upscale than "broth." Pay no mind to either word. The key is to find a brand that you like, no matter if it is called stock or broth.

VEGGIE BATTLES

As a mother, it was very important to me that my children learned to love vegetables. However, there's no sense battling with anyone over something they really, truly do not like. When they were growing up, I allowed my kids to each choose two or three things that they absolutely didn't like, and I wouldn't make them eat those things. Beyond our agreed-upon exclusions though, they had to eat every other vegetable! I found soups, especially when served with a nice, crusty garlic bread, were a wonderful way to introduce new vegetables, particularly when they were young.

STARTERS

------- SOUL FOOD --

Is there anything more soul-satisfying than a delicious homemade soup? If you've never made soup from scratch before, I promise you, it couldn't be easier. If you're already a soup connoisseur, here are two more wonderful recipes for your box.

The best thing about a soup, besides how it tastes, how it warms you up all the way down, and how it makes your house smell . . . well, that's quite a lot of good things about soup, isn't it? But another advantage is that soups can be made ahead of time, even several days before. Just reheat and add the fresh garnishes right before you serve.

I do two things to take my soup up a notch. I serve it at the table from a large tureen, and I pass a small silver tray around with fresh toppings so everyone may dress their soup as they wish. These things make the whole presentation so elegant, yet personal.

IMMERSION THERAPY

You can purée soup using your food processor or blender—be sure to leave the lid vented to allow the steam to escape—although depending upon the amount you are making, you may have to do this in batches. I find it a very messy process. It's much easier to use a hand-held immersion blender, also called a "stick blender," that allows you to whisk right in the pot.

For the garnish tray, you can use any tray you'd like of course, with beautiful small bowls. It's the passing around that everyone loves. I usually try to offer three different toppings: generally chili flakes, chopped parsley, scallions, crème fraîche, Parmesan cheese, or fresh crabmeat. If you want to be really extravagant and you've money to burn (or a truffle farm in your backyard), you can grate fresh truffle over each bowl. If not, pass around a pinch of paprika; it makes any soup look beautiful.

FOR THIS SOUP, use a combination of different exotic mushrooms, depending upon what you can find and what you prefer: chanterelles, morels, porcini or black trumpets are great options; even a simple mix of cremini mushrooms and stemmed shiitakes with dried porcini will make a wonderful soup. Mix and match them, just use anything except white button mushrooms as they have the least flavor. And buy a few really weird looking fresh mushrooms and save them to sauté and add to the soup as a final garnish.

Wild Mushroom Soup   Makes 8 to 10 servings

2 ounces dried porcini, chanterelle, morel, or black trumpet mushrooms, in any combination

6 ounces fresh mushrooms, such as cremini, chanterelle, oyster, morel, or stemmed shiitake

1 tablespoon extra-virgin olive or truffle-flavored olive oil

1 medium onion, chopped

1 garlic clove, finely chopped

2 tablespoons all-purpose flour

1 cup dry white wine

5 cups packaged organic chicken stock

Salt and freshly ground black pepper

2 tablespoons heavy cream

1. Place the dried mushrooms in a small bowl with enough boiling water to just cover the mushrooms. Let stand until the mushrooms soften, about 30 minutes. Strain soaking liquid and save 1 cup. Add the fresh mushrooms to the now-plumped dried mushrooms and chop coarsely.

2. Heat the oil in a soup pot over medium heat. Add the onion and garlic and sauté until the onion softens, about 3 minutes. Add the mushrooms and cook, stirring occasionally, until the juices evaporate, about 8 minutes.

3. Sprinkle with the flour and stir well. Stir in the cup of mushroom soaking liquid, wine, chicken stock, salt, and pepper. Bring to a boil over high heat. Reduce the heat to medium-low. Simmer for 10 to 45 minutes, depending upon how much time you have; the longer you simmer, the more robust the flavor will be, but it's still a delicious 10-minute soup! Stir in the heavy cream and heat without boiling.

4. Using an immersion blender, purée the soup in the pot until it is a porridge-like texture. Serve hot. (The soup can be made, cooled, covered, and refrigerated, for up to 1 day. Reheat before serving, adding more stock if the soup is too thick.)

White Bean Soup   Makes 8 servings

IF YOU HAVE loads of time and wish to soak your beans overnight, by all means, do so. But I don't and as I've told you, I'm all about smoke and mirrors. I've found many ways to trim time off kitchen tasks so that I can enjoy entertaining my guests. And the use of—prepare yourself!—canned beans is one of them. Not all canned beans are the same, of course. But for this recipe, good-quality organic canned cannellini beans will do the trick in a tenth of the time. You can also add shrimp; I always keep peeled, tail-on, white shrimp in my freezer to elevate any dish. Serve with fresh garnishes. If you can, grate fresh white truffle over the soup when serving.

1 tablespoon extra-virgin olive oil

1 medium red onion, chopped

2 medium celery ribs, chopped

2 garlic cloves, minced

5 cups packaged organic chicken stock

Four 15-ounce cans white beans (cannellini), drained, rinsed under cold water, and drained again

¾ teaspoon dried thyme

2 tablespoons heavy cream

2 tablespoons truffle-flavored olive oil

Salt and freshly ground black pepper

2 tablespoons finely chopped fresh parsley

1. Heat the olive oil in a soup pot over medium heat. Add the onion, celery, and garlic and cook, stirring occasionally, until softened but not browned, about 5 minutes.

2. Add the stock, beans, and thyme and bring to a boil. Reduce the heat to medium-low and simmer, uncovered, stirring occasionally, for 15 minutes. Add the cream and truffle oil and season with salt and pepper. Heat to warm the cream, but do not boil.

3. Using an immersion blender, purée the soup in the pot. Garnish with fresh parsley. Serve hot. (The soup can be made, cooled, covered, and refrigerated, for up to 1 day. Reheat before serving, adding more stock if the soup is too thick.)

TRUFFLE LOVER

I'm a huge truffle fan because I lived in the south of France for so many years. Of course, fresh truffles are hard to find and frightfully expensive, but you can get the same delicious earthy taste cooking with truffle oil, or using truffle salt or truffle butter.

55

Shepherd's Pie

Makes 8 servings

I CAN SAY THIS without hesitation: I make the best, the *absolute best* shepherd's pie. Ken will back me up on this one; it's his favorite! (The secret is in the layering.) It will melt in your mouth and warm your heart. Your man will fall in love with you all over again. Your kids will beg for more. This recipe is great for Cozy Days, but also Sexy Days and Lazy Days, as it's wonderful for days and days reheated!

While shepherd's pie is traditionally made with lamb, I make mine with ground sirloin. Use the leanest sirloin you can find. ("Cottage pie" uses ground beef as well, but instead of mashed potatoes, you lay sliced potatoes on top like the roof of a cottage.) I very often make two pans at once to have lots of leftovers for another meal. I would serve this with a green vegetable and a full-bodied, robust red wine like a Cabernet Sauvignon.

I'm also giving you my recipe for homemade mashed potatoes. I'm separating it not only because we'll be using it again for another recipe in the book, but you'll also want to use these mashed potatoes as an accompaniment to so many other dishes.

1 tablespoon olive oil

1 large onion, chopped

2 medium carrots, cut into ½-inch dice

2 garlic cloves, finely chopped

2 pounds ground sirloin (less than 10 percent fat)

One 28-ounce can diced tomatoes in juice

½ cup hearty red wine

½ cup packaged organic chicken stock

2 tablespoons tomato ketchup

Salt and freshly ground black pepper

One 11-ounce can vacuum-packed corn, drained and rinsed

Mashed Potatoes (page 58)

¼ cup freshly grated Parmesan cheese

Fresh parsley, for garnishing

1. To make the filling, heat the oil in a Dutch oven or flameproof casserole over medium heat. Add the onion, carrots, and garlic and cook, stirring occasionally, until the onion softens, about 3 minutes. Add the ground sirloin and increase the heat to high. Cook, stirring occasionally and breaking up the meat with the side of a spoon, until it loses its raw look, about 10 minutes. Stir in the tomatoes with their juices, wine, and chicken stock and bring to a boil. Reduce the heat to medium and cook at a brisk simmer, stirring often, until the juices are thickened, about 30 minutes. The mixture should be moist, but not runny. Stir in the ketchup. Season with salt and pepper.

2. Prepare mashed potatoes. While the potatoes are cooking, position a rack in the center of the oven and preheat to 375°F. Lightly oil a 9 × 13-inch baking dish.

3. Spread half of the filling in the baking dish and sprinkle with half of the corn. Top with half of the potatoes. Repeat with the remaining filling, corn, and potatoes. Sprinkle with the Parmesan. Place the baking dish on a large baking sheet.

4. Bake until the topping is golden brown, about 30 minutes. Let stand 10 minutes. If you wish, sprinkle with fresh parsley. Serve hot.

Mashed Potatoes

4 pounds baking potatoes, peeled and cut into chunks

4 tablespoons (½ stick) unsalted butter

⅔ cup whole milk

Salt and freshly ground black pepper

1. Put the potatoes in a large pot, and add enough salted water to cover them by 1 inch. Cover the pot and bring to a boil over high heat. Reduce the heat to medium-low and simmer until the potatoes are tender, about 25 minutes. (Do not undercook the potatoes, or you'll get lumps, and we want nice, creamy mashed potatoes for our topping.)

2. Drain the potatoes well. Return the potatoes to the cooking pot and cover with a clean kitchen towel. Let stand for 5 minutes. (The towel will absorb the steam from the potatoes and make them drier for a fluffy mash.)

3. Using an electric mixer on high speed, whip the potatoes with the milk and butter until smooth. Season with salt and pepper.

Chicken Paprika

Makes 6 servings

THIS IS CLASSIC European comfort food, Hungarian-style. Made from dried, ground chili peppers, paprika is frequently used to spice up dishes in Europe. I find it is underappreciated and underused in the States. Embrace this lovely red spice by using it for more than just deviled eggs! Sprinkle it over soups, salads, or any meat dish instead of using plain old black pepper.

I find chicken leg quarters are best for stewing as they don't dry out as quickly as chicken breasts. This dish is wonderful served with egg noodles.

6 chicken leg quarters, trimmed of excess skin and fat

1½ teaspoons salt and ½ teaspoon freshly ground black pepper, plus more to taste

2 tablespoons olive oil

2 medium red onions, chopped

2 garlic cloves, minced

2 tablespoons all-purpose flour

2 tablespoons sweet Hungarian paprika

⅛ teaspoon cayenne pepper

1 pound ripe red tomatoes, seeded and chopped

1 pound yellow tomatoes, seeded and chopped

1 cup packaged organic chicken stock

2 medium green bell peppers, seeded and cut into ¼-inch-thick strips

¾ cup sour cream, at room temperature

1. Preheat oven to 325°F.

2. Season the chicken with the salt and the pepper. Heat the oil in a large, ovenproof skillet over medium-high heat. In batches, add the chicken and cook, turning occasionally until browned, about 5 minutes. Transfer to a large, deep baking dish or roasting pan large enough to hold the chicken in one layer (although the pieces can overlap slightly).

3. Add the onions and garlic to the skillet and reduce the heat to medium. Cook, stirring occasionally, until the onion is translucent, about 3 minutes. Sprinkle in the flour, paprika, and cayenne and stir well. Stir in the red and yellow tomatoes and stock. Bring to a boil, stirring occasionally. Cook until tomatoes give off their juices, about 10 minutes. Pour the sauce over the chicken. Cover tightly with aluminum foil.

4. Bake for 30 minutes. Uncover, stir in the green pepper, cover again and continue baking until the chicken shows no sign of pink when pierced at the bone, about 30 minutes more. Season the sauce with salt and pepper.

5. Stir the sour cream well in a small bowl. Drizzle over the chicken mixture and serve.

59

THIS IS ONE of my most treasured recipes—one I have written down in my little pink leather-bound book. My family loves it, especially Max, and I love serving it to them. It's dead easy and tastes brilliant!

Honey Roast Pork Tenderloin with Apples

Makes 6 to 8 servings

Two 1¼-pound boneless pork tenderloins, fat trimmed

3 small garlic cloves, each cut into 10 slivers

1 teaspoon finely chopped fresh rosemary, plus more for garnishing

½ teaspoon dried thyme

½ teaspoon salt

½ teaspoon freshly ground black pepper

4 tablespoons unsalted butter, divided

3 tablespoons honey

4 Granny Smith apples, unpeeled, cored and cut into ½-inch-thick wedges

1 tablespoon cider vinegar

1 tablespoon light brown sugar

1. Position a rack in the center of the oven and preheat to 375°F. Lightly oil a large flameproof roasting pan. Using a thin-bladed knife, trim away the thin membrane on the tenderloin. Fold over the thin end of each tenderloin and tie in place with kitchen string (this gives the tenderloin an even thickness and keeps the ends from overcooking). You can even use unwaxed dental floss to do this.

2. Roll the garlic slivers in the rosemary to coat them. Using the tip of a small sharp knife, pierce 15 slits in each tenderloin, and insert a rosemary-coated sliver in each one. Combine the thyme, salt, and pepper (and any leftover rosemary) and rub all over the tenderloins.

3. Heat 1 tablespoon of butter in a large, nonstick skillet over medium-high heat. Add the pork and cook, turning occasionally, until seared on all sides, about 4 minutes. Add the remaining 3 tablespoons butter and the honey and cook, turning the tenderloins occasionally, until the mixture has reduced to a glaze, about 4 minutes.

4. Transfer the tenderloins to the roasting pan and drizzle the glaze on top. Toss the apples, vinegar, and brown sugar in a bowl and spread around the tenderloins. Bake until an instant-read thermometer inserted in the center of either tenderloin reads 145°F, about 20 minutes. Transfer the pork and apples to a platter and cover with aluminum foil. Let stand while making the sauce.

5. Place the roasting pan over high heat. Add ¼ cup water and bring to a boil, scraping up any browned bits in the pan. Boil until reduced by half, about 3 minutes.

6. Remove the kitchen string and carve the tenderloins into ½-inch-thick slices. Pour the sauce over the tenderloins and apples, and garnish with fresh rosemary. Serve at once.

61

BECOMING A MOTHER

To be a mother is God's greatest gift and deepest challenge. You are suddenly catapulted into a job where it's a matter of life and death that you get it right. You start with zero experience. You work long hours, unpaid, with lots of overtime. And you wouldn't change it for the world.

When I first held Pandora I remember thinking, "What do I do with her?" Twenty-four hours later I thought, "What would I do without her?" When I look at her face, I see her father's eyes—the eyes that I fell in love with. She has traits of us both and yet is as individual as a solitary rose.

We adopted Max when he was six weeks old, and the bonding experience was completely different. Ken and I visited Max in Wisconsin when he was first born—I remember it was snowing quite hard—but we needed to return a second time after all the paperwork. We didn't want to leave Pandora twice, so Ken went to pick up Max alone. I will never forget 6-year-old Pandora and me waiting at LAX for her daddy who was carrying very precious cargo that would ultimately change our lives. Suddenly they arrived, weary from an emotional day, and there Max was in his basket, unaware of the magnitude of his journey.

While there was no nursing or surge of hormones, it was an easy emotional transition to love this boy. We became a family right away—Pandora believed he was "hers." They are as close as any blood siblings, of that I am certain. I know in my heart there is no difference in the strength of my love for either of them. However they develop I know they are secure in the fact that, whatever direction they choose, I am right behind to catch them if they fall.

Cauliflower Gratin   Makes 6 servings

I LOVE "CAULIFLOWER CHEESE." It's a staple in Britain, like macaroni and cheese is in America. When I was a struggling single actress in London, I lived on it. It's inexpensive, easy to cook, and comforting. As with any cheesy dish, it isn't diet food, but it is extremely satisfying, and cauliflower has less calories than pasta. For a truly stellar dish, use an imported British farmhouse cheddar.

1 cauliflower, broken into bite-sized florets

4 tablespoons unsalted butter, divided, plus more for the baking dish

3 tablespoons all-purpose flour

2 ½ cups whole milk, heated

2 cups (8 ounces) sharp cheddar cheese, divided

1 teaspoon dry mustard, preferably Colman's

Salt and freshly ground black pepper

¼ cup fresh bread crumbs

1. Position a rack in the center of the oven and preheat to 400°F. Lightly butter a 9 × 13-inch baking dish.

2. Bring a large pot of salted water to a boil over high heat. Add the cauliflower and cook until barely tender, about 5 minutes. Drain, rinse under cold running water, and drain again. Pat dry with paper towels.

3. Meanwhile, melt 3 tablespoons of butter in a medium saucepan over medium-low heat. Whisk in the flour and let bubble without browning for 1 minute. Gradually whisk in the milk and bring to a simmer, whisking almost constantly. Simmer, whisking constantly, until smooth and lightly thickened, about 5 minutes. Remove the saucepan from the heat. Add 1½ cups of cheddar and the mustard. Whisk until the cheese melts. Season with salt and pepper.

4. Spread the cauliflower in the baking dish. Top with the cheese sauce. Sprinkle with the bread crumbs and remaining ½ cup cheddar, then dot with the remaining tablespoon butter. Bake until the sauce is bubbling and the topping is golden brown, about 25 minutes. Serve hot.

63

I KNOW I SAID this about my Shepherd's Pie, and of course I love all my recipes, but my roasted potatoes are second to none. Nobody can beat me on these, I promise you! They are a perfect example of how a few extra minutes and an extra pot can take a common dish and make it into something that will have people asking for the recipe. These potatoes are irresistibly crunchy and golden on the outside, and meltingly tender within. All you need is baking potatoes, preferably the ugliest, dirtiest ones from the farmers' market, some good olive oil, and salt and pepper. This makes up to eight servings, suitable for serving with a roast at a dinner party or at a table full of hungry males for a weeknight family supper. But the amount can be adjusted to make perfect potatoes in any quantity.

VanderPerfect Roasted Potatoes

Makes 4 to 8 servings

8 smallish baking potatoes, such as russet, Burbank, or Eastern

¼ cup extra-virgin olive oil

Salt and freshly ground black pepper

1. Bring a large pot of salted water to a boil over high heat. While water heats, peel the potatoes and cut in half lengthwise so they resemble igloos. Add to the water and boil just until the surface softens, about 5 minutes. Drain until they are bone dry. Return potatoes to the pot and turn the heat to medium. Cook to force out excess steam, carefully turning the potatoes with a wooden spoon, until the potatoes lightly film the bottom of the pot, about 2 minutes. Transfer the potatoes to a baking sheet, flat side down, and cool until easy to handle.

2. Position a rack in the center of the oven and preheat to 400°F.

3. Using a dinner fork, scrape all sides of the potatoes, roughing and fluffing them up. Don't skimp on this step—it's the secret to perfect roasted potatoes!

4. Pour the oil into a large roasting pan. Heat the pan in the oven until very hot, about 4 minutes. Remove the pan from the oven. Place the potatoes, flat side down, in the oil in a single layer without crowding. Using a bulb baster, baste the potatoes with the oil. Shake the pan to be sure that the potatoes aren't sticking, and arrange them so they aren't touching. Return to the oven and roast until the potatoes are crisp and a lovely golden brown, about 1 hour. If the potato bottoms threaten to get too brown, flip them over. Season with salt and pepper and serve hot.

Sweet & Tart Red Cabbage   Makes 8 servings

I DON'T KNOW what it is about this vegetable, but red cabbage just looks so beautiful. It's so simple to make, and somehow just seems way more sophisticated than it is. This dish is easily kept warm without any danger of overcooking, and just as delicious reheated.

1 large head red cabbage
(2¾ pounds), cored and chopped

3 Granny Smith apples, peeled, cored, and chopped

1 medium red onion, chopped

¼ teaspoon ground cinnamon

¼ teaspoon ground cloves

½ teaspoon salt and ¼ teaspoon freshly ground pepper, plus more to taste

½ cup red wine vinegar

2 tablespoons unsalted butter, melted

½ cup packed light brown sugar, plus more to taste

1. Position an oven rack in the center of the oven and preheat to 300°F.

2. Put the cabbage, apples, onion, cinnamon, cloves, ½ teaspoon salt, and ¼ teaspoon pepper in a nonreactive Dutch oven or flameproof casserole (at least 5 quarts). Add the vinegar, butter, and 2 tablespoons water and mix well with your hands. Sprinkle the brown sugar on top. Cook over medium heat, stirring occasionally, until steaming.

3. Cover and bake, stirring after 45 minutes, until the cabbage is very tender, 1½ to 2 hours. (They get really tender and luscious at 2 hours . . . It might be worth the wait.) Season with salt and pepper.

JUST ADD SAUSAGE

If you want to make this a whole meal, add sausages. Brown the sausages first in a skillet, on the grill, or under a broiler, and then bury them in the cabbage for the last hour of cooking.

65

English Bread & Butter Pudding Makes 6 servings

THIS IS ONE of my children's favorite recipes. Simple white bread and butter are turned into a cozy, delightful dessert that's crispy on the outside and soft and lovely on the inside. It's a great way to use up stale bread as well.

6 tablespoons unsalted butter, at room temperature, plus more for the baking dish

14 slices firm white sandwich bread

2/3 cup dried currants, golden raisins, or seedless raisins

1/2 teaspoon freshly ground nutmeg, divided

3 large eggs

1/2 cup sugar

3 cups whole milk

1/2 cup heavy cream

2 teaspoons vanilla extract

1. Position a rack in the center of the oven and preheat to 325°F. Lightly butter a 9 × 13-inch baking dish.

2. Butter the bread slices on one side. Stack the slices and cut in half diagonally. Arrange half of the bread slices, buttered side up, in the dish in 2 layers, letting the slices overlap as needed. Scatter half of the currants on top and sprinkle with half of the nutmeg. Arrange the remaining bread in the dish, and add the remaining currants and remaining nutmeg.

3. Whisk the eggs and sugar together in a medium bowl until thickened and pale. Whisk in the milk, cream, vanilla, and remaining ¼ teaspoon nutmeg. Pour slowly and evenly over the bread mixture in the dish. Press the bread into the custard to be sure it is moistened, and let stand for 10 minutes.

4. Bake until the top is lightly browned and a knife inserted in the center of the pudding comes out clean, about 25 minutes. Serve warm or cooled to room temperature.

PROPER BREAD PUDDING

While I have seen a frightful lot of bread puddings thrown together with bread cubes, a proper English bread-and-butter pudding is constructed of neatly buttered and cut bread slices in a manner that would make a Saville Row tailor proud.

I BELIEVE YOU call them "cobblers" in America (and I know you ignore the "u" in favourite," but for this recipe I've brought it with me). By any name they are dead easy and simply delicious. The flexibility of ingredients means you can usually whip one up with what you already have in your pantry, making it a great Lazy Day or dear-me-I-forgot-about-dessert dessert. You can use any of your favourite fruits, just one or in combination. I love a good black cherry-and-pear crumble, but you might try mixed berries, peaches, apples, or whatever is currently in season. If you are using a particularly tart fruit, such as Granny Smith apples, add a couple of tablespoons of sugar to the fruit mixture.

My secret is to use half canned fruit and half fresh fruit, to improve the texture while cutting the cooking and prep time. You can also customize the crumble by adding nuts, sunflower seeds, or even a crunchy breakfast cereal.

Favourite Fruit Crumble   Makes 8 servings

Three 15-ounce cans pear halves in pear juice

1½ cups pitted Bing cherries or drained, canned, pitted black cherries

1½ cups granola or old-fashioned (rolled) oats

1 cup packed light brown sugar

½ cup all-purpose flour

½ teaspoon ground cinnamon

8 tablespoons (1 stick) unsalted butter, cut into tablespoons, at room temperature

Crème Fraîche (page 68), Whipped Cream (page 168), or vanilla ice cream, for serving

1. Position a rack in the center of the oven and preheat to 350°F.

2. Drain the pears, reserving ¼ cup of the juice. Slice the pears into wedges. Transfer to a 9 × 13-inch baking dish. Stir in the cherries. Add the reserved fruit juice.

3. Stir the granola, brown sugar, flour, and cinnamon together in a large bowl. Add the butter and work together with your fingertips until the mixture forms a dough, cutting in 1 tablespoon at a time. Crumble over the fruit.

4. Bake until the fruit juices are bubbling and the topping is crisp and lightly browned around the edges, about 35 minutes. Let cool for 15 minutes. Spoon into bowls, top with crème fraîche, whipped cream, or ice cream, and serve warm.

MY NANNY KAY

Growing up, I was very close to my beloved grandmother, whom I called Nanny Kay. She was everything to me: a close friend, a confidant, a second mother. She loved fruit crumbles, and I think of her every time I make this recipe.

WHIPPED CREAM

Many a dessert is made just a little bit better with a spoonful of freshly whipped cream. It should be billowing and not too sweet. Here's how to whip it up at home:

Combine 1 cup heavy cream, 1 tablespoon confectioners' sugar, and ½ teaspoon vanilla in a chilled medium bowl. Whip with an electric mixer on high speed just until soft peaks form. Do not overbeat. Cover and refrigerate until ready to serve, up to 1 day. The tiny bit of cornstarch in the confectioners' sugar will discourage the cream from separating, but if it does, just whip or whisk the cream until it comes together again.

-------- VARIATIONS --

Peach-Blueberry Crumble: Substitute three 15-ounce cans sliced peaches and 1½ cups blueberries or blackberries for the pears and cherries.

Pear-Cranberry Crumble: Substitute 1½ cups cranberries for the cherries. Add ¼ cup granulated sugar to the fruit mixture.

68

CRÈME FRAÎCHE

Perhaps you've been to a French restaurant and tasted a dreamy, creamy dollop of dairy that you just can't put your finger on. It's not tangy enough to be sour cream, and it is too buttery to be whipped cream. What could it be?

This heavenly stuff is called crème fraîche, and if you are like me, you'll throw caution to the wind and put it on everything that you can with very few exceptions. It means "fresh cream" in French, yet it is cultured, not unlike yogurt. You can buy it at natural food supermarkets and many grocery stores, and I admit it is pricey. The good news is that you can make it at home:

Whisk 2 cups heavy cream and 2 tablespoons buttermilk together in a medium saucepan. Heat over medium, stirring constantly, just until the mixture is body temperature (stick your immaculately clean finger into the mixture to test). Pour into a clean bowl and cover loosely with plastic wrap. Let stand at room temperature until it thickens to the consistency of yogurt, about 24 hours. Transfer the crème fraîche to a covered container and refrigerate for at least 24 hours, where it will continue to thicken and gain more tangy character. The crème fraîche can be refrigerated for about a week.

CHAPTER

{4}

EXY DAYS ARE for when you're entertaining a more intimate crowd, perhaps a close group of friends, or maybe just you and your sweetheart. You'll notice I've only put a couple of days in here . . .

One of the first things I ever said on *The Real Housewives of Beverly Hills* and am most remembered for, for better or worse, is the observation that: "My husband calls me a sex object. He says every time he wants sex, I object. I say to him, 'You know what? Christmas and birthdays. And it's your birthday, not mine; that's another day off.'" Ken's immediate response? "She is a very funny person."

Obviously we laugh together, and do other things together (quite a bit), or we wouldn't have been married for so long.

KEEPING LOVE ALIVE

We all remember that incredible feeling when we first fall in love—the excitement that transcends all other emotions and those feelings of passion where every part of your being feels alive . . . But how do you maintain that for 10, 20, or 30-plus years? You don't.

You can't live your entire life on that first fuse of passion, and there's no use pretending you can. The secret of a long and healthy marriage is to keep romance and communication alive by setting aside time for one another. The minute you become too busy for each other—the moment you start to take each other for granted—is when the rot sets in.

Vow to spend one special night a week together, to remind yourselves of why you chose each other. You don't have to go out. Stay in, send the kids to bed, unplug the TV, light a candle, put on some music, serve a gorgeous dinner, and you're all set.

The Queen's English

In England, we use different words and pronunciations for both food and sex than you do in America. I can't very well share my tips for sexy entertaining if you can't understand me. So here's a quick guide to the delightfully down-and-dirty:

SEXY WORDS

Snog – To kiss someone, although frequently it means a bit more, what you would call "making out."

Shag – Very simple, it means to have sex.

FOOD WORDS

Aluminium – The silvery foil that makes kitchen clean-up a snap has an extra letter and extra syllable across the pond. We pronounce it "al-you-min-EE-um." You should, too.

Aubergine – What you would call an "eggplant," we call by its French name, pronounced "oh-burr-ZHEEN."

Courgette – By its Italian name, it's a zucchini. By its French and British name, "core-ZHET."

Filet – For reasons unknown, we don't side with the French on this one, but America does! We pronounce it "FILL-et" with the hard "t," rather than the French-y "fill-LAY."

I think very much of life is sexy—certainly preparing a delicious meal for someone you love, or even someone you just want to shag, I suppose. For me, sexiness isn't about over-the-top, showing all you've got right out of the gate. It's much sexier to keep some things a secret, to reveal them bit by bit (naughty bits last, please).

Much of life is sexy— certainly preparing a meal for someone you love —*Lisa Vanderpump*

Setting the mood for a sexy meal is almost as important as the meal itself. Keep the lighting very low and romantic: candlelight or, even better, dine only by firelight. Think outside the dining room. A sexy dinner can be eaten anywhere—the more intimate the location, the better. Gather large pillows from around your house and toss them around on the floor and eat right in front of the fire, Moroccan-style. Cover a coffee table with some sexy fabric and serve your meal there.

Of course, a sexy meal won't be very much fun if you're not there to enjoy it. With the recipes I've selected, you'll be in the kitchen less, so you can get yourself ready for a good night of fun. I've chosen absolute winners to any man's heart— hearty meat and potatoes, roasted salmon, sweet and spicy shrimp, and a quite decadent dessert meant for . . . well, I'm sure you'll figure out something. Make these and your man will give you anything you want, trust me.

I'm going to start you off with some no-fuss recipes so you can get out of the kitchen and in on the action.

CHOCOLATE OBSESSION

I freely admit I am obsessed with chocolate. I have a sinfully delicious, single piece of chocolate every day. I can't go without it. What kind you ask? It's better I don't tell you. I'm saving you, really.

Brie & Parma Ham Crostini   Makes 12 servings

KEN LIKES STRAIGHT meat and cheese, but you can sneak in some healthy greens as well (or leave out the prosciutto and go full vegetarian). Roasted asparagus or tart green apple slices would taste divine here. Use this recipe as a starter and customize as you wish.

2 tablespoons extra-virgin olive oil

1 garlic clove, minced

12 slices ciabatta bread

7-ounce round Brie cheese, rind removed, cut into 24 thin wedges

4 ounces thinly sliced prosciutto

2 teaspoons chopped fresh rosemary

1. Position the broiler rack about 6 inches from the source of heat and preheat the broiler. Combine the oil and garlic in a small bowl. Brush both sides of the bread with the garlic oil. Arrange on a broiler rack. Broil, turning once, until lightly browned on both sides, about 1 minute per side. You may have to do this in batches. Remove from the oven.

2. Top each bread slice with equal amounts of the Brie and prosciutto, then sprinkle with the rosemary. In batches, broil until the cheese begins to melt, about 2 minutes. Serve warm.

Dimitrius Salad & Feta Dressing

Makes 6 servings

THIS IS A TREASURED family recipe that we serve at Villa Blanca. Kyle Richards and I make time to have lunch or dinner together every couple of weeks, and she nearly always orders the Dimitrius Salad. It's a very sexy salad, a wonderful combination of sweet and salty. If you can find it, use French feta cheese, as it is not as harsh tasting as Greek feta. You'll start by preparing the dressing.

Feta Dressing

⅓ cup (about 2 ounces) crumbled feta cheese, preferably French

⅓ cup red wine vinegar

1 tablespoon Dijon mustard

1 tablespoon sugar

1 garlic clove, minced

1 teaspoon fresh lemon juice

¼ teaspoon dried oregano

¾ cup extra-virgin olive oil

Salt and freshly ground black pepper

Dimitrius Salad

3 small heads romaine lettuce, chopped into bite-sized pieces

6 ripe red tomatoes, coarsely chopped

2 Persian cucumbers or 1 English (seedless hothouse) cucumber, halved and sliced into half moons

1 large red onion, chopped

2 red bell peppers, seeded and coarsely chopped

2 yellow bell peppers, seeded and coarsely chopped

2 cups pitted kalamata olives

1 cup (8 ounces) crumbled feta cheese, preferably French

2 ripe avocados, peeled, pitted, and sliced

1. To make the dressing, mix the feta, vinegar, mustard, sugar, garlic, lemon juice, and oregano in a food processor or blender. With the machine running, gradually add the olive oil until smooth and thickened. Season with salt and pepper.

2. To serve at the table, toss the lettuce with enough of the dressing to coat in a large bowl. Combine the tomatoes, cucumbers, red onion, red and yellow peppers, and olives in another bowl, and spread evenly over the lettuce. Sprinkle with the feta cheese. Arrange the avocado slices on top. Pass the remaining dressing on the side.

Note: To serve on individual plates, toss the lettuce with the dressing in a large bowl. Divide salad amongst 6 dinner plates. Combine the tomatoes, cucumbers, red onion, red and yellow peppers, and olives. Spread an equal amount of the mixture over each salad, then sprinkle with the feta cheese. Arrange the avocado slices on top.

PERSIAN CUCUMBERS

The Persian cucumber, also known as a "mini seedless cucumber," is dark green, about 5 to 8 inches in length, and is sweeter than its larger brother, the seedless English or hothouse cucumber.

Herb-Stuffed Sirloin

Makes 6 to 8 servings

ORDER THE SIRLOIN ROAST from your butcher, because sirloin is usually cut into steaks. You want a 3-pound sirloin roast, about 3 inches thick. If the butcher ties the meat, remove the string. Be sure that the vegetables for the stuffing are finely chopped. It is best to mince the mushrooms in a food processor, but do the shallots and celery by hand, as they give off too much juice if chopped in a machine. This dish is best served with a side of Little Cross Potatoes (page 83) and Roasted Carrots with Honey Cayenne Glaze (page 84). And it's gorgeous with Yorkshire Pudding (recipe in my Holiday chapter; page 126).

2 tablespoons extra-virgin olive oil, divided

2 tablespoons unsalted butter

¼ cup finely chopped shallots

1 garlic clove, finely chopped

½ cup finely chopped cremini mushrooms

1 celery rib, finely chopped

1½ cups fresh bread crumbs

3 tablespoons half-and-half

1 tablespoon brandy

1 tablespoon finely chopped fresh parsley

¼ teaspoon dried thyme

½ teaspoon salt and ½ teaspoon freshly ground black pepper, plus more to taste

One 3-pound sirloin roast, about 3 inches thick

1 cup packaged organic beef stock

1. Heat 1 tablespoon of oil and the butter together in a medium skillet over medium heat. Add the shallots and garlic and cook, stirring often, until softened, about 3 minutes. Add the mushrooms and celery and increase the heat to medium-high. Cook, stirring often, until the mushroom juices have evaporated, about 5 minutes. Transfer to a bowl. Stir in the bread crumbs, half-and-half, brandy, parsley, and thyme. Season with salt and pepper to taste.

2. Turn the sirloin roast on a cut side. Starting at the center of the roast, using a thin, sharp knife, cut a deep, wide pocket into the roast. Make the pocket as large as you can without cutting through the three sides. Stuff the bread mixture into the pocket. Using kitchen twine and a trussing or mattress needle, sew up the pocket. Season surface of the steak with the ½ teaspoon salt and ½ teaspoon pepper. Let stand for 30 minutes at room temperature.

3. Preheat the oven to 425°F. Heat the remaining tablespoon of oil in a large ovenproof skillet, preferably cast iron, over medium-high heat. Add the roast and brown on all four sides,

79

allowing 2 minutes per side. Turn the roast, sewn side down, in the skillet. Transfer to the oven and roast, occasionally turning the roast so all four sides come in contact with the skillet, until an instant-read thermometer inserted horizontally into meat (but not the filling) reads 120°F for medium-rare steak, about 30 minutes. Remove from the oven and transfer the steak to a large, deep serving platter with the pocket slit running horizontally. Let stand for 5 to 10 minutes before carving. The temperature of the sirloin will continue to rise during this period, so that 120°F will end up near 130°F.

4. Pour the fat out of the skillet. Add the stock to the skillet and bring to a boil over high heat. Cook until reduced by half, about 5 minutes. Remove from the heat and set aside.

5. Remove the string from the roast. Carve across the grain into ½-inch-thick slices. Pour the stock over the roast and serve. If you wish, serve with horseradish and whole grain mustard on the side.

A Cut Above

I highly recommend investing in a high-quality set of steak knives. A beautiful cut of meat deserves a knife that can cut it beautifully. Choose something substantial to the touch and lovely to look at. Your steak knives should invite your guests to touch them. While there are dozens of choices for every budget, the important feature to look for is in the blade. You want a serrated knife, not a straight edge or micro-serrated edge. The latter might cut more neatly, but only at first. Eventually your hard plates will wear a non-serrated knife down to nothing.

Scottish Salmon with Maple Soy Glaze

Makes 6 servings

THIS COMBINATION OF sweet, salty, and nutty flavors is a perfect balance for this rich fish. I adore wild-caught Scottish salmon, but you can use regular salmon as well. Just start with a high-quality fillet: it should be firm to the touch, not sticky, be nice and pink, and have a seaside, not a fishy aroma. If you can, use pure maple syrup rather than pancake syrup as it has a fuller flavor.

Maple-Soy Glaze

½ cup pure maple syrup, preferably Grade B

¼ cup soy sauce

2 tablespoons peeled and finely chopped fresh ginger

1 scallion, white part only, finely chopped

Six 6-ounce salmon fillets

2 tablespoons extra-virgin olive oil

¼ teaspoon salt

¼ teaspoon freshly ground black pepper

Finely chopped scallion, green part only, for garnish

1. To make the glaze, bring the syrup, soy sauce, ginger, and white part of the scallion to a boil in a small saucepan over medium-high heat. Cook, stirring often, until reduced by about half, about 5 minutes. Pour into a bowl and let cool.

2. Build a medium-hot fire in an outdoor grill.

3. Brush the salmon all over with the oil. Season with the salt and pepper. Place flesh side down on the grill and cover. Grill until seared with grill marks, about 2 minutes. Flip the salmon and continue grilling until the salmon is barely opaque in the center when prodded with the tip of a sharp knife, about 4 minutes more.

4. Transfer each fillet to a plate (don't worry if the skin sticks to the grill, just leave it behind). Drizzle with the sauce. Sprinkle with the scallion greens and serve hot.

81

RAINY DAY RECIPES

Living in the English countryside for so many years, I dreamed of being able to walk outside and fire up the grill in November. Of course, that wasn't possible many, many months of the year. As such, most of my recipes have a "rain plan," that is to say you can easily roast them in your oven if the weather isn't cooperating (or if you have a flat with no balcony as I did when I first lived on my own in London).

If you would like to roast the salmon indoors, brush it with oil, season with salt and pepper, and place it skin side up on an oiled baking sheet. Roast in a 450°F oven for about 6 minutes, without turning the salmon, or until the fish is medium-rare.

THIS IS ANOTHER Villa Blanca specialty, although in England we call them "prawns," not "shrimp." I've looked it up and the only real difference—besides the lovely way prawns sounds over shrimp—is an overlapping abdominal flap on the creature or some such thing. In either case, this is a beautiful, simple dish. I usually serve it with grilled asparagus spears.

Sweet & Spicy Butterflied Shrimp   Makes 6 servings

2 tablespoons extra-virgin olive oil

2 tablespoons minced fresh cilantro

1 tablespoon peeled and minced fresh ginger

3 garlic cloves, minced

24 large shrimp, deveined and butterflied

1 cup mirin or sweet sherry

1 cup sake or dry sherry

1 cup sugar

1 cup soy sauce

2 teaspoons cayenne pepper

2 teaspoons ground cumin

2 teaspoons ground coriander

¼ cup fresh lime juice

1 tablespoon tomato purée

1. Mix the olive oil, cilantro, ginger, and garlic in a small bowl. Pour over the shrimp and marinate for 30 minutes.

2. In a small saucepan, bring mirin and sake to a simmer over medium heat. Remove the saucepan from the heat and carefully light alcohol with a long match or lighter. Let burn for 30 seconds, and cover tightly to extinguish the flames. When flame subsides, stir in sugar, soy sauce, cayenne pepper, cumin, coriander, lime juice, and tomato purée. Stir until sugars are dissolved. Remove from heat.

3. Heat grill to medium-high heat. Grill the shrimp for 3 minutes per side. (You could also bake them in a 350°F oven for 6 to 8 minutes, until they turn pink.) Remove from grill, toss shrimp with glaze, and serve.

SIDES

Little Cross Potatoes   Makes 8 servings

There is just something so sweet yet so sexy about these little roast potatoes with roast beef. For Sexy Days, you can definitely eat them with your fingers!

24 small red-skinned potatoes (about 1½ pounds)

1 tablespoon extra-virgin olive oil

¼ teaspoon salt

¼ teaspoon freshly ground black pepper

2 tablespoons prepared horseradish or sour cream

2 ounces sliced roast beef, cut into 24 pieces

Sliced fresh chives, for garnish

1. Position a rack in the center of the oven and preheat to 400°F.

2. Toss the potatoes and oil on a rimmed baking sheet to coat the potatoes. Sprinkle with the salt and pepper.

3. Bake until the potatoes are tender, about 25 minutes. Using a sharp paring knife, cut a shallow X into each potato. Squeeze the potato from the sides to open up the X.

4. Top each potato with a dab of horseradish or sour cream, then a piece of roast beef. Sprinkle with chives and serve warm.

83

JUST A GIGOLO . . .

Mistress wanted me to tell you why she named me "Gigolo." She says it's because I'm a "little sexy man" who is paid for love and affection by an older woman. She pays me with returned love and affection, as well as food, custom-made clothes, and a brilliant canopy bed by the pool! Now if only I didn't have to share her with that guy Ken who lives with us . . . Woofee! —*Giggy*

Roasted Carrots with Honey Cayenne Glaze

Makes 6 servings

SWEET AND SPICY at the same time, these are almost addictive. Serve them as a side dish, and they could steal the show from the main course! Nibble a carrot towards the end of roasting time, and if you'd like the glaze more peppery, sprinkle with additional cayenne.

Cooking oil spray

6 large, plump carrots

3 tablespoons honey

2 tablespoons extra-virgin olive oil

⅛ teaspoon cayenne pepper, plus more to taste

Salt

1. Position a rack in the center of the oven and preheat to 425°F. Line a rimmed baking sheet with aluminum foil for easy cleanup, and spray with the oil.

2. Cut the carrots into sticks about ½-inch thick and 3 to 4 inches long. Whisk the honey, oil, and cayenne pepper in a medium bowl. Add the carrots and mix to coat. Spread in a single layer in the baking sheet.

3. Roast, stirring occasionally, until the glaze has reduced, thickened, and darkened and the carrots are tender, about 25 minutes. Season with salt and additional hot pepper, if desired. Serve hot.

THE BIG "O"

I go for organic food whenever I can—preferably locally grown—but depending upon the season and where you live, fresh organic isn't always possible. But for pre-packaged ingredients, like boxed chicken stock or canned fruit, I always choose organic. Not only is organic healthier, many non-organic packaged ingredients include MSG, to which I am highly allergic. I puff up like a blowfish! Not beautiful under any circumstances . . .

IS THERE ANYTHING sexier than a juicy, roasted tomato? I think not. When tomatoes are at the peak of the summer season, these are incredible, but truth be told, they are wonderful with hothouse winter tomatoes, too.

Slow-Roasted Tomatoes   Makes 8 servings

4 large tomatoes

2 garlic cloves, thinly sliced into slivers

¼ teaspoon dried thyme

¼ teaspoon dried oregano

Salt and freshly ground black pepper

2 tablespoons extra-virgin olive oil

1. Position a rack in the center of the oven and preheat to 300°F.

2. Cut each tomato in half horizontally through its equator. Divide the garlic slivers among the tomatoes, pressing them into the seed pockets. Sprinkle with the thyme and oregano, then season with salt and pepper. Place the tomatoes, cut sides up, on a rimmed baking sheet and drizzle with the oil.

3. Roast until the tomatoes are very tender but still hold their shape, and the tomato juices are thick and concentrated, about 2 hours. Serve warm or let cool to room temperature.

MORE THAN A CO-STAR

You thought I was going to talk about my *Housewife* co-stars, didn't you? Naughty. They are all lovely ladies, and I love them dearly. I just wanted to let you know that these tender tomatoes, whose flavor has been intensified from long, low roasting, are endlessly versatile. You can certainly serve them as a side dish, but you could also chop them up and toss with cooked pasta, fresh basil, and cheese (goat cheese, Parmesan, or ricotta) for an easy supper. Or serve them with tossed greens for a light lunch. I like to make a large batch and keep some on hand in the fridge, covered and drizzled with olive oil.

85

Flourless Chocolate Cake Makes 6 to 8 servings

YOU COULD CALL this cake "the little black dress" of desserts. It is pretty easy to make, keeps for a couple of days for make-ahead entertaining, and can be dressed up with all kinds of "accessories," from whipped cream to ice cream to fresh fruit and edible flowers, or a combination. The cake can be prepared up to 2 days ahead, covered with plastic wrap and stored at room temperature. If you refrigerate it, the cake gets a fudgy texture. It's great either way.

All-purpose flour, for the pan

7 ounces high-quality semisweet chocolate, chopped

14 tablespoons (1¾ sticks) unsalted butter, cut into tablespoons, at room temperature, plus more for the pan

4 large eggs, separated, at room temperature

1 cup sugar, divided

Whipped Cream (page 68) or vanilla ice cream, for serving

Fresh raspberries, sliced strawberries, edible flowers, or a combination, for serving

1. Position a rack in the center of the oven and preheat to 375°F. Butter and flour the inside of an 8-inch springform pan, tapping out the excess flour.

2. Melt the chocolate in the top part of a double boiler over very hot but not simmering water, stirring occasionally. One tablespoon at a time, whisk the butter into chocolate until smooth. Remove the top part of the double boiler from the heat.

3. Beat the egg yolks and ½ cup of sugar in a medium bowl with an electric mixer on high speed until pale yellow and thick, about 1 minute.

4. Add to the chocolate mixture and fold in with rubber spatula. Using clean beaters, beat the whites in another bowl with the mixer on high speed until soft peaks form. A tablespoon at a time, beat in the remaining ½ cup sugar until the whites form stiff, shiny peaks. Stir about one-fourth of the whites into the chocolate mixture to lighten it, then fold in the remaining whites. Scrape into the springform pan and smooth the top.

87

5. Place the cake in the oven and immediately reduce the oven temperature to 350°F. Bake until the cake is well-puffed (it will look like a soufflé and threaten to spill over the sides, but it won't), the cracks in the top have lost their raw look, and a long wooden skewer inserted into the center of the cake comes out with moist crumbs, about 40 minutes.

6. Transfer the pan to a wire cooling rack and let cool for 5 minutes. The cake will sink. Run a sharp knife around the inside of the pan and let it cool completely. Remove the pan sides. Slice the cake and serve with a dollop of whipped cream, a small scoop of ice cream, and a spoonful of fresh fruit.

Note: If you don't want to go the double boiler route, you can use a glass bowl and a skillet. Place the chocolate in a heatproof medium bowl. Fill a skillet with about ¼ inch of water and bring to a bare simmer over low heat. Place the bowl in the water, being sure that water doesn't splash into the chocolate. Let the chocolate melt, stirring occasionally. Whisk in the butter, one tablespoon at a time. Remove the bowl from the water.

88

EDIBLE FLOWERS

When I'm entertaining at home and at my restaurants, I love to put edible flowers—specially raised without pesticides—on each plate as a colorful garnish. You can now find them at most grocery stores, and are usually packaged in combinations of pansies, orchids, and nasturtiums. You can even order them online "crystallized"—covered with sugar that makes them last for up to a year.

THIS IS ANOTHER DISH that is so easy that it has no right being so delicious. The berries are slowly baked to concentrate their flavor, and they give off their juices to mingle with balsamic and sugar to create a luscious sauce. It may take an hour or so to bake, but truthfully the hardest part of this recipe is scooping the ice cream.

Slow-Baked Strawberries with Chocolate

Makes 6 servings

2½ quarts fresh strawberries

⅔ cup sugar

⅓ cup balsamic vinegar

1½ quarts vanilla ice cream, for serving

Two 3.5-ounce bars bittersweet or semisweet chocolate, finely chopped

1. Position a rack in the center of the oven and preheat to 250°F.

2. Using a paring knife, hull each berry, then cut off the top so it stands upright. Arrange the berries, pointed sides up, in a baking dish just large enough to hold them in a single layer. Sprinkle with the sugar and vinegar.

3. Bake until the berries are tender and the juices are slightly reduced, about 1¼ hours. Let cool slightly.

4. Scoop the ice cream into serving bowls, and top with the berries and their juices, and a good sprinkling of chocolate.

LET YOUR OVEN DO THE WORK

I love baking things. There's almost nothing easier than slicing something, sticking it on a tray, and letting the oven turn it into a juicy delight. Roasted vegetables are a favorite. And I do bake peaches, generally for crumbles. But very few people know you can slow-bake strawberries to superb results. I dare you to not feel amorous after biting into one of these!

89

CHAPTER

{ 5 }

Days to Impress

HERE ARE TIMES when we're entertaining that we don't want to be too intimate or too casual. In fact, certain guests or celebrations dictate the opposite: Nothing less than an elegant, formal dinner will do. These are the Days to Impress.

On occasion, formal dinners are gatherings of our friends and family to honor once-in-a-lifetime events: a dear daughter's engagement, a special personal or business anniversary, a unique calendar event. But most of the time, formal dinners are thrown for important strangers, bosses, heads of state—let's be honest, people we want something from. In any case, it's the time to bring out the good china, splurge on quality ingredients, and make sure everyone is on their best behavior.

-------- THE MENU . . . FRAMED --------------------------------

One of the things I always do for formal parties is to write out the menu by hand on a nice piece of paper, and slip it inside a handsome photo frame. I have a large silver frame just for this purpose. Everyone loves to see the entire menu laid out ahead of time in such a personal way. And the menus are a wonderful keepsake for you—a nice reminder of lovely evenings past as well as a bit of historical reference for what you've served before.

ERRANT FOOD ETIQUETTE

While it might not seem like good manners to point it out, always tell someone if they've got a bit of food in their teeth or on their face. Not telling them is so much worse. You don't want your friend—if she really is your friend—sitting there laughing with spinach stuck in her veneers. It's not kind.

Of course, be discreet. Just lean over and whisper in her ear. Or if it's a formal evening and you can't reach her, take her aside: "Darling, I have to show you something in the other room . . ."

Once Upon a Millennium

One of the most delightful formal dinner parties I ever hosted was with friends and family to ring in the new millennium in the year 2000. It's certainly an event that only comes around every 1,000 years, so we went for it. We were living in the English countryside at the time, and I hosted a feast for 24. The set-up was sumptuous: red velvet tablecloths, votives everywhere, steaming plates of food on silver platters, cakes rimmed with flowers. It really felt like the only thing missing was Henry VIII himself!

It certainly looked like I had, but I didn't splash out a fortune at all. I didn't rent anything or buy anything special. I got creative and did it all myself. For the tablecloths, I bought two pieces of red velvet and sewed them together, added tassels on the ends, and topped it off with a fabulous gold table runner to cover the seam. I decorated the table with everything I could find in my house: little picture frames, strands of pearls, anything I thought would add to the visual feast.

I was also very clever when it came to feeding two dozen people. While I provided the main course, dessert, and drinks, that was all I did. To take the pressure off myself as hostess, I had one prerequisite for attending: every couple had to arrive with one dish that served 24 on a silver platter. (Of course, it didn't have to be real silver! Who can tell anyway, when a plate is covered in food?) Not a potluck, mind you. This was everyone bringing a stunning appetizer. My guests went all out because they only had one dish to do. It became a competition among them that we all benefitted from with an amazing 12-course meal. It became a sumptuous feast with exquisite tasters: oyster shells filled with crab salad, tiny quiche, extra large shrimp wrapped in prosciutto.

Every dish was passed around the table and became a conversation starter in itself. People were having fun talking about each other's food. It went on for hours. It was one of my most successful parties, more so because it didn't cost a bomb, and it was *so* easy.

Lobster, Crab & Mango Salad
Makes 6 servings

LOBSTER, CRAB, AND MANGO—enough said! This wonderful combination is refreshing and light; a perfect start to a formal menu. Buy the shellfish meat at the best fishmonger in town.

Mango Vinaigrette

²/₃ cup thawed frozen mango purée or canned mango nectar

¹/₃ cup rice wine vinegar

1 tablespoon plus 1¹/₂ teaspoons sugar

¹/₂ cup extra-virgin olive oil

Salt and freshly ground black pepper

Salad

2 ripe mangoes

12 cups mixed salad greens

3 cups baby arugula

3 ripe red tomatoes, chopped

12 ounces cooked lobster meat, cut into bite-sized pieces

12 ounces cooked crabmeat, picked over for cartilage and shells, cut into bite-sized pieces

9 yellow teardrop or cherry tomatoes, cut into halves

1. To make vinaigrette, process the mango purée, vinegar, and sugar in a food processor or blender. Gradually add olive oil until smooth and thickened. Season with salt and pepper.

2. Peel and pit the mangoes. Cut 1 mango into ¹/₂-inch cubes, and thinly slice the remaining mango.

3. To serve at the table, toss the salad greens, arugula, chopped tomatoes, and cubed mangoes with the vinaigrette in a large bowl. Arrange the lobster and crabmeat on the top. Garnish with the sliced mangoes and tomato halves.

Note: To serve on individual plates, toss the greens, arugula, chopped tomatoes, and cubed mangoes with the vinaigrette in a large bowl. Divide salad amongst 6 dinner plates. Top with equal amounts of the lobster and crab. Arrange the sliced mangoes on top, and garnish with the tomato halves.

95

THESE TINY BUCKWHEAT PANCAKES are the food of Russian royalty. And topped with smoked salmon (or caviar, if you can), they will definitely be fit for your fine guests! This recipe makes a lot of blini, but you can freeze them. They are good to have on hand when you need quick hors d'oeuvres for surprise guests. Do try to use buckwheat flour, as it provides the blini with the right tanginess.

Blini with Smoked Salmon   Makes 60 blini, about 12 servings

1 cup all-purpose flour

¾ cup buckwheat
or whole wheat flour

½ teaspoon salt

1¼ cups whole milk

¾ cup buttermilk

½ cup (1 stick) unsalted butter,
melted, plus more for the pan

3 large eggs, separated,
at room temperature

1 tablespoon fresh lemon juice

1 cup Crème Fraîche (page 68)
or sour cream, as needed

6 ounces sliced smoked salmon,
cut into 60 strips

2 tablespoons finely sliced fresh chives

1. To make the blini, whisk the all-purpose flour, buckwheat flour, and salt together in a large bowl. Whisk the milk, buttermilk, melted butter, egg yolks, and lemon juice together in another bowl. Pour into the flour mixture and whisk just until smooth. Do not overmix.

2. Whip the egg whites with an electric mixer on high speed until soft peaks form. Stir about one-quarter of the whites into the batter to lighten the mixture. Add the remaining whites and fold them in.

3. Heat a large nonstick skillet over medium-high heat. Lightly grease the pan with melted butter. (Do not spray with oil, as the spray builds up on the skillet and eventually ruins the nonstick coating.) Using a tablespoon for each blini, spoon the batter into the skillet. (If the batter is too thick, stir in a little more whole milk.) Cook until the underside is browned, about 1½ minutes. Turn and brown the other side, about 1 minute more. Transfer to a plate. Let cool. (The blini can be made up to 1 month ahead, separated with waxed paper, wrapped tightly and frozen. Defrost before serving.)

4. To serve, top each with a small dollop of crème fraîche, a strip of smoked salmon, and a sprinkle of chives.

BUYING BLINI

If you're in a pinch for time, you can buy pre-made blini—usually stocked in the freezer section.

The word "blini" is actually plural. A single one is called a "blin."

Beef Wellington

Makes 6 to 8 servings

THIS VERY BRITISH DISH is one of my favorites because it looks so elegant, but it is not that difficult, I promise you. Although it requires a few components, it can be readied for the oven a few hours ahead, and as long as you use a meat thermometer, always comes out in medium-rare glory to the well-deserved awe of your guests. My version uses a little truffle oil (what else?) to pump up the flavor.

Beef

One 3-pound beef tenderloin

1 tablespoon extra-virgin olive oil

2 teaspoons finely chopped fresh thyme

Salt and freshly ground black pepper

Mushroom Duxelles

1¼ pounds cremini or baby bella mushrooms, coarsely chopped

1 tablespoon unsalted butter

1 garlic clove, finely chopped

2 tablespoons finely chopped fresh parsley

1 teaspoon truffle-flavored olive oil

Salt and freshly ground black pepper

Pastry

All-purpose flour, for rolling out the pastry

One 17.3-ounce package frozen puff pastry sheets, thawed

6 ounces store-bought liver pâté

1 large egg, beaten

Madeira Jus

¾ cup Madeira

¾ cup packaged organic beef stock

2 tablespoons cold unsalted butter

1 teaspoon truffle-flavored olive oil

97

1. To prepare the beef, fold the pointed ends back and tie in place to make a solid cylinder of meat. Rub the beef with the oil, then season with the thyme, salt, and pepper.

2. Heat a very large skillet (large enough to hold the beef), preferably nonstick, over medium-high heat. Add the beef and cook, turning occasionally, until browned on all sides, about 5 minutes. Transfer to a baking sheet and let cool completely. Set the skillet with the pan juices aside.

3. To make the duxelles, add the mushrooms in batches, pulsing 8 to 10 times in a food processor until they are minced. They should almost look like a paste. Add the butter and garlic to the reserved skillet and cook over medium-high heat until the garlic softens, about 1 minute. Add the mushrooms and cook, stirring often, until their juices evaporate and the mixture is quite dry, about 12 minutes. Stir in the parsley and truffle oil and season with salt and pepper. Transfer the duxelles to a bowl and let cool completely.

4. To assemble the Beef Wellington, lightly flour a work surface. Overlap the pastry sheets by about ¼ inch. Dust the top with flour and roll out into a 19 × 12-inch rectangle, removing the creases and sealing the overlap in the process. Crumble and spread the liver pâté in a rectangle equal to the size and width of the beef in the center of the pastry, leaving a wide border of exposed pastry all around the pâté. Top with about half of the mushroom mixture. Remove the strings from the beef. Place the beef on the mushrooms. Press the remaining mushrooms on the top and sides of the beef as best as you can. Using a pizza wheel, trim 1½ inches from each short end of the pastry. Place the trimmed pastry on a plate and refrigerate uncovered until ready to bake.

WHAT IS MUSHROOM DUXELLES?

A mixture of finely minced mushrooms popular in French cooking that is created by sautéing the mushrooms in butter and then reducing them to a flavorful paste. It's pronounced "dook-SEHL."

5. Line a baking sheet with parchment paper or buttered aluminum foil. Brush the edges of the pastry with the beaten egg, reserving the remainder. Fold and enclose the pastry around the beef into a packet, pressing the seams closed. Roll the pastry-covered beef onto the baking sheet, seam-side down. Refrigerate, loosely covered with plastic wrap, until ready to bake, at least 30 minutes and up to 2 hours. Cover and chill the remaining beaten egg.

6. Position a rack in the center of the oven and preheat to 425°F. Lightly brush the pastry-covered beef with beaten egg, but do not let the egg drip onto the parchment paper. Cut the reserved pastry lengthwise into ⅛-inch strips, and use to decorate the beef in a crisscross pattern, trimming as needed. Lightly brush the strips with egg. Bake for 10 minutes. Reduce the heat to

375°F and continue baking until the pastry is golden brown and an instant-read thermometer inserted in the center of the beef reads 125°F for medium-rare meat, about 35 minutes longer. (Be sure the tip of the thermometer is truly in the center of the beef. If you have any doubts about the meat's interior temperature, believe the coolest reading that you get, as the closer the tip is to the exterior of the beef, the hotter the temperature.) Transfer to an oblong serving platter. Let stand for 15 minutes.

7. To make the jus, bring the Madeira and stock to a boil in a small saucepan over high heat. Remove from the heat. Add the butter and oil to the saucepan and whisk to dissolve the butter and lightly thicken the jus. Season with salt and pepper. Pour into a sauceboat.

8. Using a sharp, thin-bladed knife, carve the roast crosswise into ¾-inch-thick slices. (The end pieces will be medium-well, but the center pieces will be a lovely medium-rare.) Transfer to plates and serve hot, with the jus passed on the side.

Beef Wellington is believed to have been invented in the eighteenth century when many cuts of meat were wrapped in dough to keep them from scorching on the open fire while cooking. The crust kept the meat tucked within juicy and tender.

HOLLYWOOD ROYALTY

Being right in the heart of Beverly Hills, we do have quite a lot of celebrities come to Villa Blanca. Sharon Stone always sits at the same corner table. Stevie Wonder was kind enough to sing "Happy Birthday" to a nearby patron. Slash likes to put his Ray-Bans on Giggy (Giggy is such a sport when we dress him up!). Sylvester Stallone's daughters like to make their own pizzas with our chef. Fellow ex-pat Gerard Butler is a dreamy diner, even when he has to hop over trashcans to grab a car out back to avoid the paparazzi (he still gets snapped). Kim Kardashian comes in frequently with her mother Kris; they are absolutely beautiful women, especially in person.

But the most charming guest of all has to be Sir Sidney Poitier. He comes in regularly, and on a recent visit, MTV's *The Hills* was filming in our restaurant at the same time. Here sat this debonair actor, true Hollywood royalty, quietly in a corner, while on the other side of the room were three young reality stars. The girls were surrounded by cameras, paparazzi were trying to snap them through the windows, and everyone ignored the man who is truly an icon. I was touched to watch this extremely polite, well spoken, and amazing man conduct himself honorably in the midst of reality TV drama! He is really just an example to us all.

THIS JUST LOOKS SO BEAUTIFUL, especially when you carve it at the table. And it tastes divine. Garnish your serving plate with components of the stuffing: lemon slices, walnuts, and a dash of paprika. Each of your guests will only get a spoonful of the spiced rice stuffing, but it is rich enough that I assure you they won't need more than that.

Persian Chicken   Makes 6 servings

¼ cup long-grain rice, such as basmati

4 tablespoons (½ stick) unsalted butter

1 small onion, chopped

1 teaspoon sweet paprika

½ teaspoon ground cumin

½ teaspoon ground turmeric

⅓ cup seedless raisins

⅓ cup finely chopped walnuts

1 lemon, cut in half crosswise

½ teaspoon salt and ¼ teaspoon freshly ground black pepper, plus more to taste

One 6-pound chicken, giblets and excess tail fat removed

1. Position a rack in the center of the oven and preheat to 400°F.

2. Bring a medium saucepan of salted water to a boil over high heat. Add the rice and boil, like pasta, until tender, about 17 minutes. Drain in a wire sieve and rinse under cold water.

3. Meanwhile, melt the butter in a small skillet over medium heat. Transfer half of the melted butter to a small bowl and set aside. Add the onion to the skillet and cook, stirring often, until golden, about 5 minutes. Add the paprika, cumin, and turmeric and stir for 15 seconds. Remove from the heat and stir in the rice, raisins, and walnuts. Season with salt and pepper.

4. Rub the inside of the chicken with a lemon half, squeezing the lemon to release its juice. Stuff the body cavity with the rice mixture. Using a loop of kitchen string, tie the wings to the sides of the chicken. Tie the ends of the drumsticks together with another piece of string. Squeeze the juice from the remaining lemon half over the chicken. Rub the chicken all over with the reserved butter, and season with the ½ teaspoon salt and ¼ teaspoon pepper. Place a piece of foil over the exposed rice stuffing.

5. Place the chicken on a roasting rack in a roasting pan. Add ½ cup water to the pan. Roast, basting every 30 minutes or so, until an instant-read thermometer inserted in the thickest part of the thigh not touching a bone reads 170°F, about 1¾ hours.

6. Let stand at room temperature for 15 minutes. Pour the pan juices into a gravy separator, let stand 3 minutes, and pour off the drippings, discarding the fat. (Or pour the pan juices into a small glass bowl, let stand 3 minutes, and skim off the fat.) Carve the chicken and serve with the rice stuffing and a drizzle of the pan juices.

Grilled Portabellas with Herb Marinade

Makes 6 servings

YOU CAN SERVE these as a plated first course, but they are also excellent with goat cheese and maybe some roasted red pepper on crusty toasted bread as a sandwich.

102

Herb Marinade

3 garlic cloves

3 tablespoons chopped fresh parsley

3 tablespoons fresh lemon juice

2 teaspoons dried thyme

1 ½ teaspoons dried oregano

¾ teaspoon dried sage

¾ teaspoon dried rosemary

¾ teaspoon dried basil

½ teaspoon salt

¼ teaspoon freshly ground black pepper

½ cup extra-virgin olive oil

Grilled Portabellas

6 very large portabella mushroom caps, wiped clean

6 cups baby arugula

12 turkey bacon slices, cooked

1 cup (4 ounces) crumbled rindless goat cheese

Crushed hot red pepper flakes, for garnish

1. For the marinade, fit a food processor with the metal chopping blade. With the machine running, drop the garlic through the feed tube to mince the garlic. Add the parsley, lemon juice, thyme, oregano, sage, rosemary, basil, salt, and pepper. With the machine running, gradually add the oil to make a thick marinade. (Or, purée all of the ingredients in a blender.) Pour into a shallow glass baking dish.

2. Add the mushrooms and turn to coat with the marinade. Let stand at room temperature for 30 minutes, turning occasionally.

3. Build a medium-hot fire in an outdoor grill.

4. Lightly oil the grill grates. Remove the mushrooms from the marinade. Place on the grill and cover with the grill lid. Grill for 4 minutes. Flip the mushrooms, cover, and continue grilling until tender, about 3 minutes more. Transfer to a plate. Serve immediately, or cool to room temperature.

5. To serve, place a mushroom on a dinner plate. Add a handful of arugula and top with a crisscross of turkey bacon. Sprinkle with the goat cheese and a few hot pepper flakes.

Truffle Mashed Potatoes

Makes 8 servings

THIS IS A WONDERFUL WAY to introduce the flavor of truffles without the expense of fresh truffles. If you have some, by all means, grate them over the top. But your guests never need know you only used truffle butter.

4 pounds baking potatoes, such as russet, Burbank, or Eastern, peeled and cut into 1 ½-inch chunks

⅓ cup whole milk

¼ cup heavy cream

One 3-ounce container truffle butter, at room temperature

2 tablespoons unsalted butter, at room temperature

Salt and freshly ground pepper (preferably white pepper)

1. Place the potatoes in a large pot and add enough salted water to cover by 1 inch. Cover the pot and bring to a boil over high heat. Reduce the heat to medium-low and simmer until the potatoes can easily be pierced with the tip of a small sharp knife, about 25 minutes. Drain well.

2. Return the potatoes to their cooking pot. Cover with a clean kitchen towel and let stand for 5 minutes. (The towel will absorb the excess steam.)

3. Heat the milk and cream together in a small saucepan over medium heat until simmering (or heat in a microwave-safe bowl in a microwave oven). Add the truffle butter and unsalted butter to the potatoes. Mix with an electric mixer on high speed, adding as much of the milk mixture to give the potatoes your desired texture (they should be snowy with no lumps). Season with salt and white pepper. Serve hot.

103

MASH TIPS

The key to excellent mashed potatoes is patience. First, do not rush the boiling of the potatoes (and be sure that they are baking potatoes with brown jackets), as they must be nice and tender, but not mushy. And drain them really well, until they are as bone dry as you can make them. Then return them to the still-hot pot to release excess steam before mashing for the fluffiest results.

THESE LITTLE FRUITS are insanely rich and have a delicious, honeyed, juicy texture. Fresh figs are delicate. It can be hard to find an unblemished one in the store. Thankfully, we're roasting them, so they don't need to look that pretty. Slightly wrinkled but still plump figs are perfectly wonderful (can you see why I love figs so?). Even split figs are fine, as long as they are not weeping from the splits. Skin that looks a little worn is the sign of a more flavorful fig than an underripe one with taunt, shiny skin. For this dish, I recommend using a Gorgonzola piccante (also called Mountain Gorgonzola), which is drier and more crumbly than the creamy Gorgonzola dolce.

Roasted Figs with Gorgonzola   Makes 6 servings

Olive oil, for the baking dish

12 ripe figs, stems trimmed, cut in half lengthwise

½ teaspoon finely chopped fresh thyme

¼ teaspoon freshly ground black pepper

4 ounces Gorgonzola piccante, cut into 24 pieces

3 cups watercress leaves

3 tablespoons high-quality honey, preferably Greek wildflower

3 tablespoons red wine vinegar

1. Position a rack in the center of the oven and preheat to 425°F. Lightly oil a 9 × 13-inch baking dish.

2. Arrange the figs, cut side up, in the baking dish. Sprinkle with the thyme and pepper. Bake until the figs are slightly bubbling, about 6 minutes. Remove from the oven. Press a piece of Gorgonzola into each fig. Return to the oven and bake until the cheese is bubbling, about 3 minutes.

3. For each serving, mound ½ cup of watercress in the center of a plate. Arrange warm fig halves, cheese side up, around the watercress. Whisk the honey and vinegar together, and drizzle over the figs. Serve immediately.

104

Summer Fruit Bruschetta *Makes 6 servings*

THIS IS ANOTHER DESSERT that you can make in minutes, but feels special. Use whatever fresh fruit you have on hand, aiming for a colorful combination that looks as delicious as it tastes. Stone fruits (fruits with a central pit or "stone," such as apricots, peaches, and plums) work best because they can be roasted without losing their shape. My favorite combination is apricots and black cherries. And yes, in a pinch, you may sneak in some canned or frozen fruit. Look for a bread that will give you fairly large, wide slices for each bruschetta, and one without too many holes in the crumb, lest the fruit fall through.

3 ripe nectarines and/or peaches, or 6 plums and/or apricots, or a combination

24 pitted Bing cherries or canned pitted black cherries, drained

2 tablespoons orange-flavored liqueur, such as Grand Marnier

2 tablespoons sugar, plus more for topping

½ teaspoon vanilla extract

3 tablespoons unsalted butter, at room temperature

6 wide slices of crusty bread

Crème Fraîche (page 68) or Whipped Cream (page 68), for serving

1. Position a rack in the center of the oven and preheat to 400°F.

2. Halve and pit the stone fruit. Cut larger fruit (such as peaches) into eighths, and smaller fruit (such as plums) into quarters. You'll want 24 fruit slices. Toss the fruit, cherries, liqueur, 2 tablespoons sugar, and vanilla in a medium bowl. Let stand for 20 to 30 minutes.

3. Butter the bread slices and place, buttered side up, on a large baking sheet. Arrange equal amounts of the fruit and cherries over the bread slices, and drizzle with the juices. Sprinkle a little sugar on top.

4. Bake until the edges of the bruschetta are crisp and lightly browned and the fruit is tender, about 25 minutes. Transfer each bruschetta to a plate, top with a dollop of crème fraîche, and serve warm.

THIS IS ONE of our signature desserts at Villa Blanca. The secret of a creamy crème brûlée is to cook it in a covered water bath, letting the steam gently poach the delicate, rich custard. The custard can be made up to 2 days ahead, and stored in the refrigerator until ready to serve. You'll need a butane kitchen torch to create the caramelized topping.

Lavender Crème Brûlée   Makes 6 servings

3 cups heavy cream

1 bag lavender tea

8 large egg yolks

8 tablespoons sugar, divided

2 teaspoons vanilla extract

18 fresh raspberries

6 small fresh mint sprigs

1. Position a rack in the center of the oven and preheat to 325°F.

2. Heat the cream and tea bag together in a medium saucepan over medium heat until small bubbles appear around the edges of the cream. Remove from the heat and let stand 10 minutes, keeping tea bag in. Remove tea bag, pressing to extract flavor.

3. Whisk the egg yolks and ⅓ cup plus 1 tablespoon of sugar together until thickened and pale, about 1 minute. Gradually whisk the tea-flavored hot cream and vanilla into the egg yolk mixture. Strain mixture through a wire sieve into a 1-quart measuring cup. Pour equal amounts of the custard into 6 ramekins.

4. Place ramekins in a roasting pan. Pour hot water into pan so water reaches ¼ of the way up the side of the ramekins. Cover pan with aluminum foil. Cut 5 slits in foil to vent steam. Carefully place pan in oven, trying not to spill any water into ramekins. Bake 45 to 50 minutes until the middle of the crème brûlée is just firm; don't overcook as custard will firm more as it cools. Remove ramekins from hot water and let cool. Cover each ramekin with plastic wrap and refrigerate until chilled, at least 2 hours, and preferably 12 hours.

5. Just before serving, sprinkle 1 teaspoon of the remaining sugar evenly over each custard. Using a kitchen torch held closely to the sugar, pass the flame over the sugar to melt and caramelize it. Let cool until the caramel hardens. Top each custard with a mint or lavender sprig. Serve immediately.

Note: If you cannot find lavender tea, you can substitute1 bag black tea, such as Assam or English Breakfast, and ½ teaspoon dried culinary lavender. Be sure to use *culinary* lavender, now sold in jars at many supermarkets in the spice section, and not the sprayed lavender intended for potpourri.

DRINKS

A Vodka Bar

ONE OF THE THINGS I like to do at formal dinner parties is have a vodka bar. For VIP parties, I would try and get the best vodka you can. I'm not sure how many people can actually tell the difference, but it does make guests feel special to see the premium labels.

Get a few regular bottles, but also some flavored vodkas: raspberry, citron, vanilla, chocolate. With beautiful glasses and mixers—fruit juice, tonic, club soda, lemonade, lemon-lime soda—you can make dozens of different delightful drinks.

CHAPTER

{ 6 }

NE OF THE BENEFITS of living in different countries is getting to experience the local holidays. While Christmas has always been a big feast for us no matter where we lived, and Easter too, there are quite a few differences between holidays in Britain, France, and the United States.

In Britain, our biggest holiday of the year, bigger even than Christmas, is New Year's Eve. That is the day you'd better be with your family over your friends, or there'll be hell to pay. As a family, you visit your other friends all around town after "the bells," or the stroke of midnight, which is traditionally celebrated in your own home. The sort of travelling party goes on well past dawn. I'm always a bit homesick when New Year's rolls around.

We also celebrate the day after Christmas, which we call Boxing Day. It is a day for charity—boxing up your extra gifts for the poor. It was traditionally a foxhunting day, but now that the shops open up for New Year sales, it has become more of a bargain-hunting day. It's also a day for family, to go on country walks, watch sports, or play games.

In France, Christmas Eve is the biggest family holiday of the year. You fast all day, go to midnight mass, and then have a huge nighttime feast called *le reveillon*. In our house, we still have our Christmas feast after midnight mass.

WORKING BACKWARDS

For me, the key to staying organized during huge holiday cooking events—without having to get up at 4 a.m.—is to work backwards. The day before, I get a sheet of paper and put down the exact timing of everything, starting with when I want to serve the food and working backwards. For instance, if I want to serve at 3 p.m., the turkey must be out at 2:20 p.m. so I can let it rest before carving, the potatoes must go in at 2 p.m., and so forth.

The day before Lent, called Fat Tuesday in America, is Shrove Tuesday in Britain. Our biggest tradition is eating pancakes for dinner that day, preferably with lemon and sugar. It came about as people made huge batches of pancakes hoping to use up all of their milk, butter, and eggs because they used to be forbidden food during Lent.

We don't celebrate Thanksgiving in Britain, but I must admit, it's a lovely holiday and I really do enjoy it. Any chance to get together with family and concentrate on what we're thankful for is a wonderful idea.

I think it's very important to give back to those who are less fortunate. I am acutely aware that life has blessed me in many ways, so I endeavor to put a little piece back into this jigsaw puzzle we call life. Since the day we opened Villa Blanca, every Monday we deliver food to homeless shelters. I like to personally drive the food over, and I don't just drop it off, I get out of my car and serve it myself. I make it a point to get to know people and call them by their first name. I feel it's important; it might be the only time anyone talks to them that day. It's such an easy thing to do to help restore dignity to someone.

When I see the lines of people waiting for food, it is a humbling experience knowing that many have simply lost their way in life, perhaps have undiagnosed mental disorders, or are losing a battle to addiction. There but for the grace of God go any one of us.

It doesn't matter what you do, just do something. Be kind. Help another. However small, it all adds up. If everyone does just one thing, it will make a difference. And I guarantee you will draw more from the experience than you will ever give.

Sausage Rolls with Cranberry Sauce

Makes 30 bite-sized rolls, enough for about 8 servings

SAUSAGE ROLLS ARE a traditional British holiday appetizer, although if you cut them large enough, they can suffice as a meal in and of themselves. You might also want to serve with an accompaniment of English mustard (in a pretty bowl, of course—no bottles allowed!).

Cranberry Sauce

One 12-ounce bag fresh or frozen cranberries

1 cup orange juice

½ cup sugar

¼ teaspoon ground cinnamon

¼ teaspoon ground cloves

Sausage Rolls

1 pound bulk pork sausage

1 medium onion, finely chopped

¼ teaspoon dried sage

¼ teaspoon dried thyme

One 17.3-ounce package frozen puff pastry sheets, thawed

All-purpose flour, for the work surface

1 large egg, well beaten

1. To make the cranberry sauce, bring the cranberries, orange juice, sugar, cinnamon, and cloves to a simmer in a nonreactive medium saucepan over medium-high heat, stirring to dissolve the sugar. Reduce the heat to medium and simmer, stirring often, until the cranberries have given off their juices and are lightly thickened, about 7 minutes. Transfer to a bowl and let cool. (The sauce can be made up to 3 days ahead, covered and refrigerated. If too thick, thin with additional orange juice.)

2. To make the sausage rolls, position a rack in the center of the oven and preheat to 400°F. Line a large baking sheet with parchment paper or a nonstick baking mat (or use a nonstick baking sheet).

3. Mix the sausage, onion, sage, and thyme together in a medium bowl. Unfold the pastry sheets and place on a lightly floured surface with the folds running vertically. Cut each sheet vertically into thirds along the folds for a total of 6 strips. Divide the sausage mixture into 6 equal portions. Shape 1 portion of the mixture in a log down the length of a pastry strip. Very lightly brush one long edge of the strip with the beaten egg. Bring the long ends of the strip together to meet over the sausage mixture, and pinch the seam closed. Transfer to a small, unlined baking sheet, seam side down. Repeat with the remaining puff pastry and sausage mixture. Freeze or refrigerate for 15 minutes.

4. Use a sharp knife to cut each pastry roll into five 2-inch pieces. Brush each roll lightly with some of the beaten egg. Pierce the top of each twice with the tip of the knife. Place on the lined baking sheet, seam side down. Bake until puffed and golden brown, 25 to 30 minutes. Do not underbake. Serve warm, with the cranberry sauce in a bowl with a spoon so guests can add a dab of sauce on their roll before eating.

Sausage rolls taste best when they are freshly baked, but they can be prepared up to 1 day ahead, covered and refrigerated. Reheat in a preheated 350°F oven for 10 minutes.

COOK WITH OIL, BAKE WITH BUTTER

When selecting puff pastry at the store, look for one that lists butter in the ingredients, not oil. Butter will give your pastry a lighter, crispier crust.

THIS HAS BECOME somewhat of a modern classic, thanks to my dear friend Frozen Puff Pastry. I like the combination of sweet-tart cherry preserves with the buttery Brie, but you can also use your favorite fruit chutney for a more savory flavor. And yes, you can eat the rind, so don't bother trimming the cheese.

Brie en Croute
Makes 8 to 10 servings

¼ cup sliced natural almonds

1 sheet (half of a 17.3-ounce package) frozen puff pastry, thawed

All-purpose flour, for rolling out the dough

One 13- to 14-ounce round ripe Brie, cut in half horizontally

½ cup cherry preserves

1 large egg beaten with 1 teaspoon water, for glazing

Water crackers, for serving

1. Preheat the oven to 350°F. Spread the almonds on a baking sheet. Bake, stirring occasionally, until lightly browned, about 8 minutes. Let cool. Position a rack in the center of the oven. Turn oven up to 400°F.

2. Place the pastry on a lightly floured work surface and dust the top with flour. Roll out into an 11-inch square, removing the creases in the dough.

3. Place the bottom half of the Brie, cut side up, in the center of the pastry. Spread with the preserves, then sprinkle on the almonds. Set the top half of the Brie, cut side down, on the cherry-almond filling. Bring up the pastry to completely cover the Brie, cutting off and reserving excess pastry. Place the pastry-covered Brie, seams down, on an ungreased baking sheet. Refrigerate, with the reserved pastry scraps, for 10 minutes.

4. Using a small sharp knife, cut the pastry scraps into decorations. (For example, cut the pastry into leaf shapes, and use the tip of the knife to mark with veins.) Lightly brush the pastry-covered cheese with the egg mixture, add the pastry decorations, and brush again.

5. Bake until the pastry is golden brown, 20 to 25 minutes. Let cool for 10 minutes. Transfer to a serving platter and serve hot, with the crackers.

117

BUYING BEAUTIFUL BRIE

When buying Brie, look for one that is just a little under-ripe: It should be firm and smell sweet. A wheel of Brie that is overripe—has a spongy rind and smells a bit of ammonia—will not cook up well. Another trick: Stick the Brie in the freezer for 30 minutes before you prepare it. It will still cook beautifully, but not be too runny when you cut into it.

Roast Turkey with Lattice Bacon and Pork and Walnut Stuffing

Makes 8 to 10 servings with leftovers

THERE ARE A LOT of ways to cook a turkey, but my version has tricks to add extra moisture to give you a juicy, tasty bird. In Britain, we traditionally layer bacon slices—we call them "rashers"—over our turkey to make it extra juicy while it's roasting. I like to weave mine into a little lattice pattern, but you can just lay them across however you'd like. You can use toothpicks to help keep the bacon in place.

Pork and Walnut Stuffing

6 tablespoons (¾ stick) unsalted butter

1 large onion, chopped

4 celery ribs, finely chopped

1 pound bulk pork sausage

6 cups fresh bread crumbs

1 cup coarsely chopped walnuts

¼ cup chopped parsley

¾ teaspoon dried thyme

Salt and freshly ground black pepper

Roast Turkey

One 12- to 14-pound fresh turkey

4 tablespoons unsalted butter, at room temperature

1 teaspoon salt

½ teaspoon freshly ground black pepper

8 bacon slices

1. To make the stuffing, melt the butter in a large skillet over medium heat. Add the onion and celery and cook, stirring often, until softened, about 5 minutes. Add the sausage and cook, breaking up the meat with the side of a spoon, stirring often, until the meat is cooked through, about 10 minutes. Transfer the sausage mixture and its juices to a large bowl. Add the bread crumbs, walnuts, parsley, and thyme, and season with salt and pepper.

2. Position a rack in the bottom third of the oven and preheat to 425°F.

3. Remove the giblet packet; set aside. Rinse the turkey inside and out with cold water and pat dry with paper towels. Loosely fill the neck cavity with the stuffing, and pin the neck skin to the back skin with a skewer. Loosely fill the body cavity with the stuffing. (Do not cram the stuffing into the turkey, as it expands during cooking.) Transfer any remaining stuffing to a buttered 11 × 8½-inch baking dish, cover with foil, and refrigerate. Rub the turkey top and sides with the butter. Season the outside of the bird with the salt and pepper. Place the turkey on a roasting rack in a large roasting pan. Arrange the bacon in a crisscross pattern over the turkey breast. Cover the roasting pan with a double thickness of aluminum foil (extra-wide heavy-duty foil works best), tenting the foil slightly so it doesn't touch the turkey.

4. Roast for 30 minutes, then reduce the oven temperature to 350°F. Bake for 1¾ hours. Remove the foil. Continue roasting until the turkey is browned and an instant-read thermometer inserted in the thickest part of the breast reads 175°F, about 45 minutes more. Transfer the turkey to a platter, tent with aluminum foil, and let stand for 30 minutes before carving. Place the refrigerated stuffing in the oven and bake until heated through, about 30 minutes.

5. Carve the turkey and serve with the gravy (page 121) and stuffing, including the stuffing in the baking dish.

BIGGER BREASTS

Whenever I'm to roast a turkey, I always buy the full bird plus an extra breast. Let's be honest, the breast is what everyone wants anyway, and this way, the best meat is ready on time, and I never run out. I cook the turkey breast at 350°F for about an hour, then slice it up, add it to the roast turkey carvings, and cover it with gravy, and no one is the wiser. In fact, the extra breast allows me to purchase a smaller whole turkey, which in turn saves me having to get up at dawn to dress it and get it into the oven.

I also use the turkey drippings from the smaller breast to make the first batch of gravy. Knowing you have a perfect turkey breast and gravy ready to go takes a huge amount of pressure off the cook!

A Kinder, Gentler Gravy

IF YOU HAVEN'T the heart (or stomach) to make a gravy from the giblets, you're certainly not alone. They package the insides into a nice white bag so that people can easily throw it away without actually looking at it for a reason. I do want to save you from buying just a jar of prepared gravy however, so here is a homemade gravy that uses some of the juicy drippings and chicken stock.

Turkey drippings from pan

3 ½ cups packaged organic chicken stock

8 tablespoons (1 stick) unsalted butter

½ cup all-purpose flour

½ cup white wine

Salt and freshly ground black pepper

1. Pour the pan juices from the roasted turkey into a 1-quart gravy separator. Let stand for 5 minutes to let the fat rise to the top. Pour off the turkey drippings into a 2-quart measuring cup; discard the turkey fat. (If you don't have a gravy separator, you can use the 2-quart measuring cup and simply spoon the fat off the top.) Add enough stock to make 1 quart.

2. In a medium saucepan, melt the butter. Whisk in the flour, then the wine. Whisk over medium heat for 3 minutes. Whisk in the stock mixture and bring to a boil, stirring often. Reduce the heat to medium-low and simmer, whisking often, until thickened, about 10 minutes. Keep the gravy warm over very low heat. If the gravy gets too thick, add more stock or water. Season with salt and pepper.

Marinated Eye of Round Roast Beef

Makes 6 servings

EYE OF ROUND, a roast that we call "silverskin" in the U.K., is a delicious and inexpensive alternative to beef tenderloin (although because I am so fond of beef tenderloin in this marinade, I've included a recipe for it, too). A very lean roast, the trick to keeping it moist and tender is to roast it no more than medium-rare, and to cut it into thin slices.

1 cup hearty red wine, such as Shiraz

½ cup balsamic vinegar

¼ cup plus 1 tablespoon extra-virgin olive oil, divided

1 tablespoon finely chopped fresh rosemary

1 tablespoon finely chopped fresh sage

2 garlic cloves, 1 chopped, 1 cut into 12 slivers

½ teaspoon salt

½ teaspoon freshly ground black pepper

One 3-pound eye of round, excess fat trimmed, but leave the silverskin intact

1 cup packaged organic beef broth

1. Combine the wine, balsamic vinegar, ¼ cup oil, rosemary, sage, chopped garlic, salt, and pepper in a 1-gallon plastic storage bag.

2. Using the tip of a sharp knife, make 12 incisions all over the beef. Insert a garlic sliver in each incision. Add the beef to the marinade and close the bag. Refrigerate, turning occasionally, for at least 1 and up to 8 hours.

3. Position a rack in the center of the oven and preheat to 450°F.

4. Remove the beef from the marinade and pat it dry with paper towels. Heat the remaining 1 tablespoon oil in a large skillet over high heat. Add the beef and cook, turning occasionally,

COOKING WITH WINE

I love to cook with wine, and sometimes I even put it in the food. Never buy one of those bottles labeled "cooking wine" in the seasoning section of the store, however; the added salt will ruin your dish. If you wouldn't uncork it and drink it with a dear friend, you shouldn't be cooking with it!

until browned on all sides, about 6 minutes. Transfer to a roasting pan. Add the beef broth to the skillet and bring to a boil, scraping up the browned bits in the pan with a wooden spoon. Set the skillet with the broth aside.

5. Roast the beef for 10 minutes. Reduce the oven temperature to 350°F. Continue roasting until an instant-read thermometer inserted in the center of the roast reads 125°F, about 1¼ hours. Transfer the roast to a carving board, tent with aluminum foil, and let stand for 10 minutes.

6. Reheat the broth in the skillet and pour the jus into a sauceboat. Using a thin, sharp carving knife, cut the roast across the grain into thin slices. Serve immediately, with the jus to pass.

-------VARIATION ---

Marinated Roast Beef Tenderloin

Substitute a 2¾-pound trimmed beef tenderloin for the eye of round. Tuck the tapered end of the beef under the rest of the roast and tie it in place with kitchen string to make a roast of even thickness. Marinate the roast and brown as directed. Preheat the oven to 450°F. Roast, without reducing the oven temperature, until an instant-read thermometer inserted in the center of the roast reads 120°F for medium-rare meat, about 30 minutes. Let stand for 10 minutes. Remove the string and carve.

123

MANY COOKS (especially in Europe) call this easy dish "Baker's Lamb," harking back to the days when the only oven in town would belong to the village baker, and people would bring their holiday roasts to cook in that oven after the bread was finished. The meat juices from the lamb infuse the garlicky potatoes with their flavor. This could become your favorite way to cook lamb, which I believe is the perfect Easter dish.

Leg of Lamb with Garlic Potatoes   Makes 6 to 8 servings

One 6-pound leg of lamb on the bone

3 garlic cloves, 1 cut lengthwise into 12 slivers, 2 smashed under a knife and peeled

1 tablespoon finely chopped rosemary

5 tablespoons (½ stick plus 1 tablespoon) unsalted butter, melted

1 teaspoon plus ¾ teaspoon salt, divided

1 teaspoon freshly ground black pepper, divided

4 pounds baking potatoes, such as russet, Burbank, or Eastern, peeled and sliced crosswise into ¼-inch-thick rounds

1. Position a rack in the center of the oven and preheat to 450°F.

2. Trim any excess surface fat from the lamb. Using the tip of a sharp knife, make 12 incisions all over the lamb. Slip a garlic sliver with chopped rosemary into each incision. Rub the lamb with 1 tablespoon of melted butter, and season with 1 teaspoon salt and ½ teaspoon pepper.

3. Place the lamb on a rack in a large roasting pan and roast for 15 minutes. Remove the pan from the oven and reduce the oven temperature to 350°F.

4. Toss the potatoes and crushed garlic with the remaining 4 tablespoons melted butter in a large bowl. Season with ¾ teaspoon salt and ½ teaspoon pepper. Remove the lamb and the rack from the pan, spread the potatoes in the pan, and put the lamb on top. Return to the oven. Continue roasting, stirring up the potatoes every 20 minutes or so, until the potatoes are golden and tender, and an instant-read thermometer inserted in the thickest part of the lamb (not touching a bone) reads 125°F for medium-rare lamb, about 1¾ hours. (If the potatoes are done before the lamb, transfer them to an ovenproof dish, cover with aluminum foil, and reheat for a few minutes before serving.)

5. Remove the lamb from the oven and transfer to a serving platter. Tent the pan with the potatoes with aluminum foil and keep warm in the turned-off oven. Let the lamb stand for 10 minutes. Transfer the potatoes to a serving dish. Carve the lamb and serve with the potatoes. If you wish, add some peas and a dollop of cranberry sauce for color.

Yorkshire Pudding

Makes 9 servings

WHEN I MENTIONED to a young American friend of mine that I was putting Yorkshire pudding in my cookbook, she crinkled her nose and said, "Don't you have any other desserts?" I know steamed puddings and fruitcakes have an undeservedly bad reputation in America, but not all puddings are desserts! Yorkshire pudding is actually a savory side dish made of batter, and traditionally served with roast beef. It's like a cross between a popover and a muffin. I'm determined that you will all start cooking them up and loving them wholeheartedly. And with this delicious mini version, I don't see how you can't!

³⁄₄ cup all-purpose flour

¼ teaspoon salt

½ cup whole milk, at room temperature

1 large egg, at room temperature

4½ teaspoons rendered beef fat from a roast, lard, or vegetable oil, divided

1. Position a rack in the center of the oven and preheat to 425°F.

2. Sift the flour and salt together into a small bowl. Whisk the milk, ½ cup tepid water, and the egg together in a medium bowl. Gradually whisk in the flour mixture and whisk just until smooth. Do not overmix. Set aside at room temperature for 30 minutes.

3. Spoon ½ teaspoon of rendered fat into each of the 9 cups in a standard 12-cup muffin pan. Place the tin in the oven and heat for 2 to 3 minutes until the pan is very hot. Remove the pan from the oven. Whisk the batter briefly and pour into a 2-cup (or larger) liquid measuring cup. Pour the batter into the 9 prepared cups, filling each about half full. Return the pan to the oven and bake until the puddings are puffed, crisp, and deep golden brown, about 20 minutes. Do not open the door until at least 15 minutes has elapsed, or the puddings could collapse. Remove the puddings from the pan and transfer to a napkin-lined basket. Serve immediately. (If the puddings soften, reheat and re-crisp them in a 425°F oven for 3 to 5 minutes.)

The perfect time to make Yorkshire Pudding is when your roast is resting (any large roast should rest for at least 20 minutes before carving). Turn up the oven and bake off some puddings!

Chestnut Stuffing   Makes 8 to 12 servings

I ADORE STUFFING and I adore scrambled eggs, and this one combines both! Perfect to accompany just about any dish for the days when you're not roasting a whole turkey. Use day-old, firm white sandwich bread so the cubes hold their shape. Squishy bread will not do. I prefer to shell fresh chestnuts, but you can use 2 cups coarsely chopped vacuum-packed chestnuts, if you wish. And yes, you can easily cut the recipe in half for smaller meals.

One 1-pound loaf firm white sandwich bread, cut into ½-inch cubes (about 10 cups)

12 ounces fresh chestnuts

8 tablespoons (1 stick) unsalted butter, plus more for the baking dish

1 medium onion, chopped

8 ounces bulk pork sausage

2 tablespoons chopped fresh parsley

1 tablespoon chopped fresh thyme

3 large eggs

¼ cup whole milk

½ teaspoon salt

¼ teaspoon freshly ground black pepper

1. The night before making the stuffing, spread the bread cubes on baking sheets and let stand, uncovered, overnight to dry the bread slightly.

2. The next day, using a very sharp paring knife, cut an X into the flat side of each chestnut. Place in a large saucepan and cover with cold water. Bring to a boil over high heat. Reduce the heat to medium-low and simmer until the chestnut flesh is tender when pierced with a knife, about 20 minutes. Remove the saucepan from the heat. One at a time, using a slotted spoon, remove the chestnuts from the water, and use the paring knife to remove the dark brown skin and lighter brown inner peel. (You can use a kitchen towel to protect your hands from the hot chestnuts. The chestnuts must be hot or warm during peeling.) Coarsely chop the chestnuts. You should have about 2 cups chopped chestnuts.

3. Position a rack in the center of the oven and preheat the oven to 350°F. Lightly butter a 15 × 10-inch baking dish.

4. Melt the butter in a large skillet over medium heat. Transfer about 6 tablespoons of the melted butter to a small bowl. Add the onion to the butter in the skillet and cook, stirring occasionally, until softened, about 3 minutes. Add the sausage and cook, breaking up the sausage with the side of a spoon, until the meat loses its raw look, about 10 minutes.

5. Transfer the sausage mixture to a large bowl. Add the bread cubes, chestnuts, parsley, and thyme. Add the reserved melted butter and mix well. Whisk the eggs, milk, salt, and pepper together, pour over the bread mixture, and stir again.

6. Spread the stuffing in the prepared baking dish. Cover with aluminum foil. Bake until the stuffing is piping hot, about 30 minutes. If you like crispy stuffing, remove the foil after baking for 15 minutes.

Brussels Sprouts with Bacon and Balsamic Vinegar

Makes 8 servings

1/3 cup slivered blanched almonds

Two 10-ounce containers Brussels sprouts, each trimmed and cut in half

1 tablespoon extra-virgin olive oil

4 bacon slices, coarsely chopped

1 medium onion, chopped

2 garlic cloves, finely chopped

1/4 cup dry white wine

2 tablespoons balsamic vinegar

Salt and freshly ground black pepper

1. Preheat the oven to 350°F. Spread the almonds on a baking sheet. Bake, stirring occasionally, until lightly browned, about 8 minutes. Let cool.

2. Bring a large pot of lightly salted water to a boil over high heat. Add the Brussels sprouts and cook until they turn a brighter shade of green, about 2 minutes. Drain and rinse under cold running water. Pat dry.

3. Heat the oil in a large skillet over medium-high heat. Add the bacon and cook, stirring often, until it begins to brown, about 5 minutes. Add the onion and garlic and cook until the onion is translucent, about 3 minutes longer.

4. Add the Brussels sprouts and cook, stirring only occasionally so they get a chance to get golden brown and crispy in spots, until the sprouts are just tender, 10 to 12 minutes. Stir in the wine and vinegar and cook until the mixture evaporates, about 2 minutes. Season with salt and pepper. Stir in the almonds. Transfer to a serving bowl and serve hot.

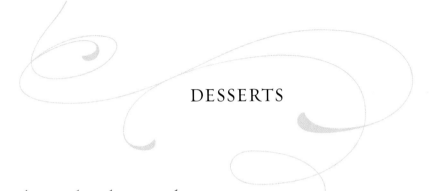

Scottish Whisky Cake   Makes 6 to 8 servings

WHAT COULD BE better than a cake made from whisky? A cake that tastes delicious for days and days . . . This can be made up to 3 days ahead, cooled, wrapped in plastic wrap, and stored at room temperature. In fact, it is even better if it ages a little. To make it, choose a mild, nicely balanced Scotch (anything with a "Glen" in the name is a safe bet), and stay away from heavy, smoky whiskies (anything from Islay or Skye). Even a blended whisky, such as Dewar's, will work, but you'll get the richest flavor from a single malt.

1 cup all-purpose flour, plus more for the pan

1 teaspoon baking powder

¼ teaspoon ground allspice

¼ teaspoon ground cinnamon

¼ teaspoon ground cloves

¼ teaspoon ground nutmeg

¼ teaspoon salt

¾ cup (1½ sticks) unsalted butter, at room temperature, plus more for the pan

¾ cup packed light brown sugar

3 large eggs, at room temperature, beaten

½ teaspoon lemon extract

¼ cup single malt Scotch whisky

1 cup seedless raisins, golden raisins, or dried currants, or a mixture

¼ cup dried cranberries or cherries

Grated zest of 1 large orange

1. Position a rack in the center of the oven and preheat to 325°F. Lightly butter and flour a 7- to 8-inch springform pan, tapping out the excess flour.

2. Sift the flour, baking powder, allspice, cinnamon, cloves, nutmeg, and salt together. Beat the butter in a medium bowl with an electric mixer on high speed until smooth, about 1 minute. Gradually beat in the brown sugar, eggs, and lemon extract, and continue beating until the mixture is pale, about 2 minutes. With the mixer on low speed, add the flour mixture in three additions, alternating with two equal additions of the whisky, and mix just until smooth, scraping down the sides of the bowl with a flexible spatula. Stir in the raisins, cranberries, and orange zest. Scrape into the prepared pan and smooth the top.

3. Bake until the cake is golden brown and a long wooden skewer inserted into the center of the cake comes out clean, about 1 hour. If the cake threatens to get too brown, tent the top with aluminum foil. Let cool on a wire cooling rack for 10 minutes. Run a knife around the inside of the pan and remove the pan sides. Invert the cake onto the rack, turn right side up, and let cool completely.

129

"RUSTIC" IS THE PERFECT word for this simple, homespun dessert. Again, it's not an American-style pudding, but a soft apple cake that creates its own sauce. Serve it warm from the oven with crème fraîche or ice cream, it just might replace apple pie as your favorite holiday dessert.

Apple Pudding Cake

Makes 8 servings

Butter, for the baking dish

1 cup plus 2 tablespoons all-purpose flour, plus more for the pan

½ cup sugar

2 teaspoons baking powder

Pinch of salt

1 cup buttermilk

1 large egg

1 teaspoon vanilla extract

3 Granny Smith apples, peeled, cored, and thinly sliced

½ cup packed light brown sugar

Crème Fraîche (page 68), Whipped Cream (page 68), or vanilla ice cream

1. Position a rack in the center of the oven and preheat to 350°F. Lightly butter and flour a 9 × 13-inch baking dish and tap out the excess flour.

2. Sift the flour, sugar, baking powder, and salt together into a medium bowl. Whisk the buttermilk, egg, and vanilla together in another bowl. Pour into the flour mixture and whisk just until smooth. Stir in the apples. Spread in the prepared baking dish. Boil 1 cup of water and stir in brown sugar to dissolve. Slowly pour around the edges of the batter in the baking dish.

3. Bake until the top of the cake is golden brown and springs back when pressed in the center, about 45 minutes. Serve the cake in bowls with its sauce, topped with crème fraîche.

DRINKS

Hot Toddy

A HOT TODDY is the perfect drink for a chilly night, made all the more perfect because you can make it with any number of things. By definition, a hot toddy is a warm cocktail that consists of three things: alcohol, sweetener, and a base such as tea or water. For your spirit, you can use whisky, brandy, bourbon, or even spiced rum (or any combination thereof). The most popular sweetener is honey, but some people use sugar. I use black English tea as the base, but you can also use hot apple cider, coffee, or even hot water.

There are dozens of variations, but here's how I make my hot toddy: Add 2 ounces of whisky to your mug. Pour in hot tea. Add a half slice of lemon, two cloves, and a cinnamon stick. Let it steep for 3 minutes.

Hot toddies have long been thought to help ease head colds and asthma, but today most doctors do officially frown on the use of alcohol for any type of home remedy. I'm at home, however, it's chilly outside, and I'm smiling with mug in hand. Cheers!

131
—

CHAPTER

{7}

Sunny Days

love holidays, and I love snuggling in on Cozy Days, but in truth, I love Sunny Days the most. I don't believe you can have too many sunny days in your life. The more the better! A lack of sunshine is one of the reasons we left the beautiful English countryside and moved to the south of France, and the almost constant sun is one of the many reasons I adore California.

Sunny Days are meant for outdoor entertaining. This is when you have your poolside parties, your barbeques, your patio lunches, and your picnics. Being outside allows you to use nature as a backdrop for your décor. Add cut flowers and buds and lots of green to your tables. Put whole fresh fruit in glass bowls. I love to use brightly colored fabrics as an accent. Instead of searching for large pieces to cover an entire table, I use several smaller pieces laid across the table's width. Filmy Indian-inspired prints are especially lovely out-of-doors.

Warm weather also begs for a different menu. The food should be lighter, preferably served cold. The menu needn't be as formal. Instead of splitting courses, allow the food to just flow together. For Sunny Days, I'm giving you all the recipes together for you to mix and match.

J'ADORE PANDORA

I named my daughter Pandora because I just loved the way the name sounded. It's beautiful and one-of-a-kind . . . just like her! I love her nickname equally as much: Pandy.

Papaya with Crab   Serves 6

THIS IS ONE OF my favorite dishes. It's so delicious and impressive-looking, perhaps because the papaya is used as a natural bowl. You can't get any more beautiful than nature! Garnish with sliced strawberries.

3 ripe papayas

¼ cup light mayonnaise

1 tablespoon fresh lemon juice

2 tablespoons fresh rosemary, chopped

⅛ teaspoon paprika

Salt and freshly ground black pepper

1 pound jumbo lump crabmeat, picked over for cartilage and shells

1 large ripe tomato, diced

1. Cut each papaya in half, then cut a strip off the opposite side so the papaya will sit on the plate nicely without rolling around. Scoop out the seeds.

2. Mix mayonnaise, lemon juice, rosemary, paprika, salt, and pepper. Carefully fold in crabmeat and tomatoes. Scoop into papaya halves and serve.

1 PAPAYA, 2 PAPAYA . . .

You'll want a perfectly ripe papaya, nice and juicy. The best way to get a good one is to ask the grocer. Tell them exactly when you want to eat it, and be specific—this Wednesday at 3:30 p.m.—and they'll help you find fruit that will be ripe at that exact time. If you can't find such an expert, look for a papaya that is still firm and green with just some yellow. It should ripen fully in about 2 days just sitting on your counter. Overripe papayas will be all yellow, soft or mushy, and smell sweet. Avoid those. And I always buy 1 more papaya than I'm going to need in case something goes wrong, for instance, if one of them is too ripe.

136

To grill chicken evenly, cook over medium-hot, not searingly hot, heat. If the fire is too hot, the chicken will burn before it is cooked through. You can also cook the chicken in a broiler for about the same amount of time. Serve with buttered basmati rice; stir in some chopped cilantro or pistachios, if you wish to make it extra lovely.

Chicken Tikka with Fresh Mango Chutney

Makes 6 servings

Chicken Tikka

2 cups plain low-fat yogurt

3 garlic cloves, finely chopped

1 teaspoon ground cumin

1 teaspoon ground coriander seeds

1 teaspoon ground ginger

1 teaspoon ground turmeric

½ teaspoon chili powder

½ teaspoon salt

2 ½ pounds boneless and skinless chicken breasts

Mango Chutney

2 ripe mangoes, peeled, pitted, and cut into ½-inch dice

2 tablespoons chopped fresh cilantro

1 teaspoon sugar

¼ teaspoon ground ginger

⅛ teaspoon cayenne pepper

Salt, to taste

1. To prepare the chicken, mix the yogurt, garlic, cumin, coriander, ginger, turmeric, chili powder, and salt together in a large bowl. Cut the chicken into 30 chunks about 1½ inches square. Add to the yogurt mixture and stir to coat. Cover and refrigerate at least 3 hours and up to 12 hours.

2. To make the chutney, combine the mangoes, cilantro, sugar, ginger, and cayenne in a medium bowl. Season with salt. Cover and refrigerate for 1 to 2 hours to blend the flavors.

3. Build a medium-hot fire in an outdoor grill. If a charcoal grill, let the coals burn down until they are covered with white ash and you can hold your hand just above the cooking grate for about 3 seconds, about 30 minutes after lighting the fire. If a gas grill, preheat on high, then reduce the heat to medium.

4. Have ready 6 metal grilling skewers. Remove the chicken from the bowl, shaking off the excess marinade. For each serving, thread 5 chicken pieces onto a skewer, leaving a little space between each piece of chicken. (For grilling, metal skewers work better than wooden ones. If you must use wooden skewers, soak them in warm water for 30 minutes, then drain. Cover the exposed "handle" end of the skewer with aluminum foil before grilling, or it will burn, even though it is soaked.) Let stand at room temperature for 15 minutes.

5. Brush the grill grate clean and lightly oil the grate. Place the chicken skewers on the grill and cover with the grill lid. Grill, turning occasionally, until the chicken is cooked through, 12 to 15 minutes. Transfer the skewers to a platter.

6. Serve the chicken hot, with the chutney passed on the side.

137

You've Got to Have Friends

Friendships play an important role in life, and if we can manage to cultivate a handful of really true loyal relationships in our time on this planet then we should be thankful. Over the years, Ken and I have surrounded ourselves with a colorful, eclectic palette of people from all walks of life.

Women especially need good girlfriends. It's been reported that women speak an average of 7,000 words daily compared to men who say only 2,000 (and my husband who uses only 200!). We just can't get the same juice from a man. I'm fairly certain the reason I have never needed therapy is because my friends have filled that gap for me. To have someone you can trust and know they have your interests at heart is a rare find; if you are lucky enough to have people in your life like that, keep them close and nurture the friendship.

The most important things I require in a friend are honesty and heart. And I think I am becoming more discriminating the older I get—I have no inclination to invest in a person who doesn't share the same values or moral compass that I do.

Ken and I have enjoyed a certain serendipity when it comes to finding friends, but in a few instances we have failed. We recently endured a painful (and sadly very public) experience of failed friendship. We included somebody into the core of our existence, let down our guard, opened our home, and allowed him into our daily lives. We treated him like family for a long time. He was masquerading as a man who loved us.

When he betrayed us, it was devastatingly hurtful and made me question my own reasoning. How could I be so naïve? How had I missed the hubris of this man who infiltrated my family? He slowly and insidiously manipulated us, and we were fools to allow him to do so. I now blame myself for not listening to my inner voice, my intuition. He inadvertently had given me so many warnings of the type of person he was capable of being, and I stupidly had ignored them. While at first I felt a gut-wrenching anger, slowly those feelings subsided. As always I started to see the humor in the situation—and I've discovered that nothing annoys your enemy so much as forgiving them!

While Ken and I closed ranks at first, we know we cannot protect ourselves from everything. We will continue to open and share our hearts and souls with strangers, and risk letting down our guard, as the reward of good friendship is well worth it.

THIS SALAD IS SO SIMPLE, yet so flavorful; perfect for a light meal. I adore it so much, I named it after my daughter. The juicy sweetness you get from the fresh peaches served with the saltiness of the prosciutto is an utter delight. The honey chile dressing adds a yin and yang that tickles the taste buds. If you have time and want to really enhance the flavor profile, grill the peaches beforehand. You can also substitute any stone fruit—apricots, plums, nectarines—for the peaches.

Pandora Salad   Makes 6 servings

Honey Chile Vinaigrette
¼ cup rice wine vinegar
3 tablespoons honey
1 garlic clove, minced
¼ teaspoon ground cayenne pepper
½ cup extra-virgin olive oil
Salt and freshly ground black pepper

6 cups coarsely chopped mâche, butter, or Bibb lettuce
3 ripe yellow peaches, each pitted, halved, and sliced into 8 wedges
1½ cups (6 ounces) shredded mozzarella cheese
3 ounces thinly sliced prosciutto
½ cup packed fresh mint leaves

1. To make vinaigrette, process the vinegar, honey, garlic, and cayenne pepper in a food processor or blender. Gradually add the olive oil until smooth and thickened. Season with salt and pepper.

2. To serve at the table, put the salad greens in a large serving bowl. Drizzle with the vinaigrette and toss. Arrange peach slices over the top, then sprinkle with the mozzarella. Drape prosciutto slices evenly over the peaches. Sprinkle with the mint.

Note: To serve in individual portions, toss the lettuce with vinaigrette in a large mixing bowl. Divide salad amongst 6 dinner plates. Arrange 4 peach slices on top of each salad, topped with ¼ cup of mozzarella. Drape each with an equal amount of the prosciutto. Sprinkle with the mint.

LAMB'S LETTUCE

If you've never had mâche lettuce, you must find it and try it. You will thank me for it. It's been popular in France for centuries, but is only just making its way over here. Also called corn salad, field lettuce, lamb's lettuce, and lamb's tongue (because it looks like little lamb tongues), its small-ish, oval leaves have a sweet, slightly nutty flavor. Sweet and slightly nutty—like a lot of my *Housewife* friends. You can see why I might enjoy it!

139

Asian Tuna Tartare with Salt-and-Pepper Crisps

Makes 6 servings

THIS IS ONE of my favorite dishes at Villa Blanca. Of course, things like this always look so lovely in restaurants, with the salads shaped into precise, professional-looking mounds. But you can do the same at home using a simple trick: a large cookie cutter. Pack the salad in the cutter, then gently lift the cutter off to leave an impressive edible tower on the plate.

18 wonton or gyoza wrappers, cut into 2-inch circles

Olive oil, for the crisps

¼ teaspoon salt and ⅛ teaspoon freshly ground black pepper, plus more to taste

¼ cup mayonnaise

2 tablespoons fresh lime juice

2 tablespoons Asian dark sesame oil

⅛ teaspoon ground coriander

⅛ teaspoon cayenne pepper

Pinch of ground caraway seeds

Pinch of ground cumin

1 pound high-quality tuna steak, cut into ½-inch cubes

2 ripe avocados, pitted, peeled, and cut into ½-inch cubes

2 tablespoons Japanese (masago or tobiko) fish eggs (optional)

2 teaspoons toasted sesame seeds

Microgreens or sprouts, for garnish

White truffle oil, for serving

1. Position a rack in the center of the oven and preheat to 375°F.

2. Arrange the wrappers closely together on a baking sheet, but do not let them touch each other. Brush the wrappers with olive oil. Combine the salt and the pepper and sprinkle over the wrappers. Bake until the wrappers are crisp and golden brown, 6 to 8 minutes. Loosen the wrappers from the sheet with a metal spatula, then let cool completely.

3. Whisk the mayonnaise, lime juice, sesame oil, coriander, cayenne pepper, caraway, and cumin together in a medium bowl. Add the tuna, avocado, fish eggs, if using, and sesame seeds, and gently fold together. Season with salt and pepper.

4. For each serving, place a 2½-inch-diameter (at least 1-inch high) cookie cutter in the center of a serving plate. Spoon one-sixth of the tuna mixture into the cutter and smooth the top with a rubber spatula. Lift off the cutter. Top with microgreens and drizzle with truffle oil. Arrange several crisps against the tartare and serve at once.

GYOZA WRAPPERS

Gyoza wrappers are round wonton wrappers, available at Asian markets and many supermarkets. If you can't find them, simply use square wonton wrappers, and cut them into rounds with a 2-inch-diameter cookie cutter.

141

THIS IS A wonderfully healthy salad that combines the crunch of pine nuts with juicy grilled chicken and "buttery" lettuce. For the sweet corn, you can use freshly cooked, but canned corn will work just as well. You can of course eat the lettuce cups like a regular salad with knives and forks, but it's also fun to pick them up and eat them with your fingers.

Char-Grilled Chicken Lettuce Cups

Makes 6 servings

3 pounds boneless and skinless chicken breast halves

2 tablespoons extra-virgin olive oil

1 ½ teaspoons salt

½ teaspoon freshly ground black pepper

¾ cup drained canned or fresh corn

¾ cup finely chopped red onion

⅓ cup pine nuts, toasted (see sidebar)

3 heads butter or Bibb lettuce, separated into 18 large leaves

2 ripe avocados, peeled, pitted, and sliced

Lemon Dijon Dressing

½ cup fresh lemon juice

¼ cup sugar

2 tablespoons Dijon mustard

1 ½ cups extra-virgin olive oil

Salt and freshly ground black pepper

1. Position the broiler rack about 6 inches from the source of heat and preheat the broiler. Brush the chicken with the oil and season with the salt and pepper. Broil the chicken, turning once, until lightly browned and an instant-read thermometer inserted through the side of a breast half into the center reads 165°F, about 12 minutes. Transfer to a plate and let cool for 10 minutes. (You can also grill the chicken breasts outside on an outdoor grill directly over medium heat for 12 to 15 minutes.)

2. To make the dressing, process the lemon juice, sugar, and mustard in a food processor or blender. With the machine running, gradually add the olive oil and process until smooth and thickened. Season with salt and pepper.

3. Shred chicken using two forks, or your fingers if you feel like getting dirty. Place in large mixing bowl. Add corn, red onion, and pine nuts. Mix with ¾ cup of the dressing.

4. For each salad, place 3 lettuce leaves on each plate. Fill the leaves with equal amounts of the chicken salad and top with the avocado slices. Pass the remaining dressing on the side.

TOASTED PINE NUTS

To toast pine nuts, cook them in a small skillet over medium heat, stirring almost constantly, until lightly browned, about 3 minutes. Transfer to a plate and let cool completely.

142

Moroccan Roasted Vegetable and Couscous Salad

Makes 8 to 12 servings

THIS COLORFUL SALAD makes a statement, especially if prepared in a large, clear bowl to show off its layers. Whether you serve it as a side dish at a grilled dinner or as a main course for lunch, it is light but full of flavor.

Dressing

¼ cup fresh lime juice

1 tablespoon tomato paste

2 teaspoons ground coriander seed

2 teaspoons ground cumin

Salt and freshly ground black pepper

¼ teaspoon cayenne pepper, plus more as needed

¾ cup extra-virgin olive oil

½ cup finely chopped fresh parsley

Roasted Vegetables

¼ cup extra-virgin olive oil, plus more for baking sheets

3 garlic cloves, chopped

Two 1⅓-pound eggplants, trimmed and cut into 1½-inch cubes

3 zucchini, cut into 1-inch cubes

1 each red, yellow, and orange bell peppers, seeded and cut into ½-inch-wide strips

1 large red onion, cut into ½-inch-thick half-moons

Salt and freshly ground black pepper

Couscous

1 tablespoon extra-virgin olive oil

½ teaspoon salt

One 5-ounce package couscous

1 ½ cups (6 ounces) crumbled rindless goat cheese

1 pint cherry tomatoes, cut into halves

½ cup coarsely chopped pitted kalamata olives

One 5-ounce package mixed spring greens

1 cup fresh parsley leaves

143

1. To make the dressing, whisk the lime juice, tomato paste, coriander, cumin, and cayenne in a medium bowl. Gradually whisk in the oil, then add the parsley. Season the dressing with salt and pepper, and, if desired, additional cayenne. (The dressing should be spicy, so don't skimp on the cayenne.) Cover and set aside.

2. Position racks in the center and top third of the oven and preheat to 475°F. Lightly oil 2 large rimmed baking sheets.

3. To prepare the roasted vegetables, mix ¼ cup of oil and the garlic in a large bowl. Add the eggplant, zucchini, bell peppers, and onion and mix to coat. Season with salt and pepper. Spread on the baking sheets. Roast, stirring occasionally and switching the positions of the sheets from top to bottom after 20 minutes, until the vegetables are tender and their edges are beginning to brown, about 40 minutes. Let cool.

4. Meanwhile, start the couscous. Bring 2 cups of water, the oil, and the salt to a boil in a medium saucepan over high heat. Add the couscous and stir. Remove from the heat and cover tightly. Let stand until the couscous is tender, about 5 minutes. Fluff with a fork, transfer to a bowl, and let cool. Break up any clumps of couscous with your fingers.

5. Choose a very large glass bowl to hold the salad, layering the ingredients against the sides of the bowl so they are visible. Spread the couscous in the bowl, and drizzle with a few tablespoons of the dressing. Top with the goat cheese, then the tomatoes and olives. Add the roasted vegetables, and drizzle with a few more tablespoons of dressing. In a separate bowl, toss the mixed greens, parsley, and remaining dressing, then heap them on top of the vegetables. Serve immediately, being sure to include all of the ingredients in each portion.

GRINDING SPICES

Spices play a big role in my cooking. I use fresh, dried, and ground. But I don't want you to have to buy dozens of bottles of each spice. You can buy just the whole dried spices and grind what you need at home as you need it. To grind them, you can hand crush the spices in a mortar and pestle, or use an inexpensive electric coffee grinder (with a propeller blade, not the burr style) that you have set aside for grinding spices instead of coffee so you don't transfer flavors.

Strawberry Shortcake Scones   Makes 8 servings

I'VE NEVER MET anybody who didn't love a good scone. (Emphasis on *good* of course; not those dry, brick-like ones sold behind too many coffee counters.) And I dare say this recipe will make the best scones you've ever tasted: tender and sweet. I usually make two batches at once—one for Ken and the children to nibble on and one for company. You may substitute a nice fruit liqueur, such as Grand Marnier, rum, or brandy for the water when sweetening the strawberries. The scones can be made up to 8 hours ahead, covered with plastic wrap and stored at room temperature.

2 quarts strawberries, sliced, plus 4 whole strawberries for garnish

¼ cup plus 1 tablespoon sugar, divided, plus more for topping scones

2½ cups all-purpose flour, plus more for work surface

2 teaspoons baking powder

¼ teaspoon salt

12 tablespoons (1½ sticks) cold unsalted butter, cut into ½-inch cubes

⅔ cup whole milk

2 large eggs

1 cup Whipped Cream (page 68)

1. Position a rack in the center of the oven and preheat to 425°F.

2. Combine the sliced strawberries, 2 tablespoons of sugar, and 2 tablespoons water in a medium bowl. Set aside to let the strawberries give off some juices, at least 20 minutes and up to 2 hours.

3. Sift the flour, the remaining 3 tablespoons sugar, the baking powder, and salt together into a medium bowl. Add the butter. Using a pastry cutter or two knives, cut the butter into the flour mixture until it resembles coarse crumbs with some pea-sized pieces of butter. Mix the milk and egg with a fork to blend. Slowly stir the milk mixture into the flour mixture just until it forms a soft dough. Do not overmix.

4. Turn the dough out onto a lightly floured work surface. Cut the dough into 4 equal pieces. Shape each into a round about 2½ inches wide and 1-inch thick. Sprinkle the tops with sugar. Place on an ungreased baking sheet. Bake until well risen and golden brown, 15 to 18 minutes. Transfer to a wire cooling rack and let cool.

5. Split each scone in half horizontally. For each serving, place a scone bottom on a dessert plate, top with a quarter of the sliced berries and cream, add the scone top, and garnish with a whole strawberry. Serve immediately.

DRINKS

Villa Blanca Raspberry Mojito

YOU KNOW I'M PARTIAL to anything pink, but there's truly nothing more refreshing on a sunny day than a raspberry mojito. There's no point in just making one, so I'm going to give you the recipe for a whole pitcher. You may add more sugar to taste. I always make sure to have extra mint leaves and whole raspberries on hand to garnish not only the pitcher, but also the tray I place it on.

⅓ cup fresh raspberries

½ cup fresh mint leaves, packed

3 limes, quartered

3 tablespoons sugar, preferably superfine or bartenders' sugar, as needed

6 ounces light rum

12 ounces club soda, as needed

1. Muddle the raspberries, mint leaves, and limes in the bottom of your pitcher with a muddler or wooden spoon. Mix in the sugar.

2. Fill a cocktail shaker halfway full with crushed ice. Add rum and shake for 10 seconds to chill. Pour into the pitcher. Add more crushed ice to the pitcher, then fill to the top with club soda.

Pimm's No. 1 Cup Cocktail   Makes 6 servings

WHILE LONG ISLAND has its alcoholic iced tea, Britain has a delicious spirited fruit punch called "Pimm's No. 1 Cup." Pimm's is a party drink, and I often serve it as the "house cocktail," with bottles of Pimm's and soda and bowls of the garnishes to allow guests to make their own. You can also add oranges and strawberries to make a "Garden Party Pimm's," but this is the classic recipe.

1 small apple, cored but unpeeled

1 lemon

1 Persian or Kirby cucumber, scrubbed but unpeeled

1¼ cups Pimm's No. 1 Cup

2½ cups lemon-lime carbonated soda

6 large mint sprigs

1. Cut half of the apple into thick wedges, and the remainder into thin slices. Do the same for the lemon and cucumber. Put the apple, lemon, and cucumber in a large pitcher.

2. Add the Pimm's Cup, then the soda. Stir gently.

3. For each drink, spoon the fruit into a tall glass. Add ice, then pour in the liquid. Garnish with a mint sprig and serve.

149

A PIMM'S PRIMER

This cocktail can be quite confusing if you don't know the terminology. So let's clear it all up while you're still nice and sober, shall we? Pimm's is a brand of bottled liqueur that is pre-mixed with fruit juices and spices (also called a "fruit cup."). Pimm's No. 1 Cup, the one you'll find most readily in the stores, has a gin base. (Pimm's No. 3 has a brandy base; No. 6 is vodka-based.) To make a Pimm's No. 1 Cup cocktail, you combine Pimm's No. 1 cup, lemon-lime soda, and fresh sliced fruit. (Yes, cucumber is a fruit, Darling.)

CHAPTER

{ 8 }

Lazy Days

HERE ARE TIMES, particularly after dark or when the weather isn't cooperating, that you must bring the informal party inside. These I call the Lazy Days. Whether you're just having girlfriends over or someone pops by unexpectedly, your meal can still be delightfully easy and simply delicious.

Of course, the presentation should still be beautiful. Any food, no matter how simple, is elevated when served on a lovely plate with fresh flowers. Even peanut butter and jelly would look wonderful with an artful arrangement—cutting the sandwich with cookie cutters and garnishing the plate with fresh fruit and nuts, for example. (Although truth be told, I would never serve peanut butter and jelly at any time to anyone. I could never eat it. We don't mix savory with sweet in one bite in the U.K. It's just not done.)

One of my best tips for entertaining on lazy days is to let your servingware do the work for you. By that I mean let them make such a statement, not much else is needed. For instance, when I'm serving a really simple meal indoors, I always try and use the largest platter I can find. Just one thing done on a grand scale will give your meal a strong impact.

I have quite a varied collection of pewter bowls, stamped platters, and enormous trays. I purchase them whenever I see them; they're quite rare and so useful. A large platter can be used for a salad, pasta, piles of sandwiches—almost anything. If you don't have a lot of storage room for oversized dishes, pop them under a bed until you need them.

Just like the food for Sunny Days, the menu needn't be formal. Who knows who might pop by? As in the last chapter, I'm giving you all the recipes together for you to mix and match.

JUST A GIGOLO. . . .

It's not just Mistress who thinks I'm fit for royalty. Pomeranians have been popular with kings and queens in Europe for hundreds of years. Queen Victoria even bred them herself. Her dogs became quite famous—not as famous as me, but they didn't have Twitter back then. She's credited with starting the craze for small Poms in the 1890s. We're still popular after all these years, and rightly so. Tum ti tum tum.
—*Giggy*

Striped Salad with Honey Balsamic Vinaigrette

Makes 6 to 8 servings

I'VE FOUND THAT when I have the girls over, they mostly want to eat just salad. Here is my divine take on a Cobb salad that is sure to impress and easy to assemble. For this to look really good though, you must serve it in as large a serving piece as you can find. An antique-looking salad bowl big enough to bathe a baby in would be ideal, but even if you only have a flat, rectangular tray, use it. We need a giant canvas for these gorgeous greens.

Honey Balsamic Vinaigrette
½ cup balsamic vinegar
2 tablespoons fresh lemon juice
2 tablespoons honey
1 cup extra-virgin olive oil
Salt and freshly ground black pepper

1 head iceberg lettuce, cored and shredded
2 heads romaine lettuce, chopped
½ pound smoked ham, cut into ½-inch cubes
3 red tomatoes, peeled, seeded, and cut into ½-inch cubes
3 yellow or orange tomatoes, peeled, seeded, and cut into ½-inch cubes
2 ripe avocados, peeled, pitted, and cut into ½-inch cubes
4 hard-boiled eggs, peeled and cut into ½-inch cubes

1 cup (4 ounces) crumbled blue cheese
One 15-ounce can corn kernels, drained and rinsed
2 small red onions, diced
¾ cup pine nuts, toasted (page 142)

155

1. To make the vinaigrette, whisk the vinegar, lemon juice, and honey in a medium bowl. Gradually whisk in the olive oil. Season with salt and pepper.

2. Mix the iceberg and romaine lettuce in a large bowl. Toss with ½ cup of the dressing. Spread the lettuce evenly over a large, deep platter or salad serving bowl.

3. Arrange the ham in a neat row on top of the lettuce in the center of the platter. Add tomatoes, avocados, eggs, blue cheese, corn, onion, and pine nuts in strips on either side of the ham. Serve with the remaining dressing passed on the side.

YOU CAN OVERCOMPLICATE any recipe, but I don't see the point. I could tell you to grow your own lentils, then pick them, and soak them, but we would be here for weeks! My version uses ready-to-go canned lentil beans (try to find organic), tastes delightful, and any lazy person can make it! As we did with our soups in Chapter 3 (page 53), serve your guests from a large tureen at the table, and pass around a pretty tray of garnishes: bowls of crushed hot pepper flakes, chopped fresh parsley, crème fraîche, Parmesan cheese, or whatever toppings you have on hand. Since it's hardly any extra work, I like to make twice as much soup as I'll need, and then freeze the extra. That way I have a quick dinner all ready for another Lazy Day.

Lazy Day Lentil Soup   Makes 6 to 8 servings

2 tablespoon extra-virgin olive oil

3 ounces chopped pancetta

1 medium red onion, chopped into half-moons

2 garlic cloves, chopped

2 quarts packaged organic chicken stock

Two 15-ounce cans lentils, drained and rinsed

One 14-ounce can diced tomatoes with juices

½ cup hearty red wine, such as Shiraz

¼ teaspoon hot red pepper flakes

Salt and freshly ground black pepper

Assorted garnishes for serving (see above)

1. Heat the oil in a large saucepan over medium heat. Add the pancetta and sauté until crispy, about 5 minutes. Add the onion and garlic and cook, stirring occasionally, until the onion softens, about 3 minutes.

2. Add the stock, lentils, tomatoes and their juices, wine, and red pepper. Bring to a boil, then reduce heat to medium-low. Cover and simmer for 10 minutes. Use an immersion blender to puree the soup to the thickness you like. Season with salt and pepper, and keep warm.

3. Serve the soup hot, allowing each guest to add toppings as they wish.

French Onion Tart

Makes 8 appetizer servings

WHEN I WAS COLLECTING my favorite entertaining recipes, I called Pandora, and she insisted I include this one. Onion tarts are very popular in the south of France, and we all grew quite fond of them when we lived there. The quiche shell is partially baked before adding the filling—otherwise, the bottom crust would be soggy. The pastry is lined with foil and weighed down with pastry weights before baking to keep the sides from falling in. Pastry weights are available at kitchen shops, or you may use dried beans or uncooked rice. (The beans and rice can be stored in an airtight container and reused as pastry weights for a few months.) Serve with a nice wine—like our Villa Blanca Sauvignon Blanc—and your guests will believe you are a posh hostess indeed.

All-purpose flour,
for rolling puff pastry

1 sheet (half of one 17.3-ounce box)
frozen puff pastry, thawed

6 bacon slices, coarsely chopped

2 large onions, chopped

3 large eggs

¾ cup whole milk

¼ teaspoon salt

⅛ teaspoon freshly ground
black pepper

⅛ teaspoon freshly grated nutmeg

½ cup (2 ounces) shredded
Gruyère cheese

1. Position a rack in the center of the oven and preheat to 400°F. Lightly butter a 9-inch-square tart pan with a removable bottom.

2. Roll out the puff pastry on a lightly floured work surface into a ⅛-inch thick rectangle, removing the creases in the pastry as you go. Fit the pastry into the tart pan, being sure to fit the pastry into the corners. Roll the rolling pin over the top of the pan to cut off the excess puff pastry. Pierce the bottom and sides of the pastry well with a fork. Cover loosely with plastic wrap and freeze while preparing the filling.

ALL SORTS OF SHAPES

I like to bake my French Onion Tart in a 9-inch-square pan because it makes the tart easy to cut into bite-sized (well, perhaps two-bite) servings. You can also use a 14 × 5-inch rectangular tart pan. If baked in a 9-inch-diameter round pan (you might not need all of the custard filling), it's best to slice the tart into wedges and serve on a plate with mixed greens.

3. Cook the bacon in a large skillet over medium-high heat, stirring often, until crisp and browned, about 8 minutes. Using a slotted spoon, transfer the bacon to paper towels. Pour off all but 2 tablespoons of the fat from the skillet.

4. Add the onions to the skillet and cook, stirring often, until softened, about 5 minutes. Reduce the heat to medium-low and cook, stirring often, until golden brown, about 15 minutes. Transfer to a large bowl and let cool until tepid. Stir in the bacon. Whisk the eggs, milk, salt, pepper, and nutmeg together in another bowl. Set aside.

5. Meanwhile, line the pastry with aluminum foil to protect from becoming too crisp. Fill with pastry weights, and place the pan on a baking sheet. Bake until the edges are lightly browned and set, 12 to 15 minutes. Remove the baking sheet and pan from the oven. Lift off the weights and remove the foil. Pierce the pastry with the fork again, return to the oven, and continue baking until the pastry is beginning to brown, about 5 minutes more. If the pastry puffs too much, just pierce it with the fork. Remove from the oven.

6. Sprinkle the cheese over the pastry. Scatter the onion mixture over the cheese, then pour in the custard, being careful not to overfill the pastry. Carefully return to the oven (if the custard spills under the pastry, it will be hard to remove the tart from the pan) and bake until the filling is evenly puffed and golden brown, about 30 minutes. Let cool in the pan for 5 minutes. Remove the sides of the pan. Cut into wedges or rectangles. Serve warm or let cool to room temperature.

Villa Blanca Wines

One of the first things Ken and I did when we decided to open restaurants in California was to seek out a local vineyard to bottle our own wines. You may have seen us on the show travelling up to Summerland for a tasting. Villa Blanca wines are our restaurant's house wines, and they will be available at stores nationally later this year.

As you probably know by now, I am very visual, and our wine had to represent the feeling of Villa Blanca—elegant, yet relaxed; European, yet accessible. I designed the bottle with a unique hand-dipped top and the Villa Blanca crest on the front. It's simple, but looks fabulous on the table.

We currently have a very smooth Cabernet Sauvignon; a crisp Sauvignon Blanc; a newly-introduced Pinot Noir; and my personal favorite, a rosé. Rosé is not as popular in the United States as it is in Europe, but I aim to change that. I am a strong advocate of rosé. There is nothing better than a chilled rosé at lunch or on a summer evening. Many rosés I find too sweet, but the Villa Blanca Rosé is made from the Grenache grape. It's simply perfect; people go crazy for it.

WE WERE ALL sitting down one day before Villa Blanca opened trying to name our dishes. We were throwing out suggestions for this delicious, but dead easy pasta. We wanted a word that would describe how beautiful it was, and "Lolita," a term we'd all heard to describe a beautiful, tempting woman, came to mind. Like a beautiful woman, simplicity is what makes this pasta super sexy and beautifully delectable, so it remained.

Pasta Lolita   Makes 4 to 6 servings

1 pound spaghetti

3 tablespoons extra-virgin-olive oil

½ cup minced red onion

3 garlic cloves, minced

2 boneless and skinless chicken breast halves, cooked and shredded

4 ripe plum (Roma) tomatoes, seeded and chopped

⅓ cup pine nuts, toasted (page 142)

1 cup dry white wine

1½ cups packaged organic chicken stock

2 packed cups baby spinach

⅓ cup freshly grated Parmesan cheese, plus more for serving

Salt and freshly ground black pepper

1. Bring a large pot of salted water to a boil over high heat. Add the spaghetti and cook according to the package directions until al dente. Do not overcook the spaghetti, as it will be cooked in the sauce.

2. Meanwhile, as soon as the pot goes on to boil, start the sauce. Heat the oil in a large skillet over medium-high heat. Add the red onion and garlic and reduce the heat to medium. Cook, stirring occasionally, until the onion is translucent, about 4 minutes. Add the chicken, tomatoes, and pine nuts. Cook until the tomatoes give off some juices, about 1 minute.

3. Add the wine and bring to a boil. Cook until the wine is evaporated to a few tablespoons, about 10 minutes. Add the stock and simmer for 5 minutes.

4. Drain the spaghetti well. Add to the chicken mixture, along with the spinach and Parmesan cheese. Stir over medium-low heat until the spinach is wilted, about 2 minutes. Season with salt and pepper. Serve in bowls, with additional Parmesan cheese passed on the side.

THIS WONDERFUL, nutritious, vegetarian pasta has a pesto-based sauce. When we added
it to the menu at Villa Blanca, we named it after the city that invented pesto: Genoa, Italy.

Spaghetti Genovese   Makes 4 to 6 servings

3 fingerling potatoes, halved lengthwise, then cut crosswise into ½-inch-thick slices

6 asparagus spears, woody ends trimmed, cut on a diagonal into ¼-inch-thick pieces

3 ounces (about 1½ cups) haricot verts or small thin green beans, ends trimmed

1 pound spaghetti

⅓ cup extra-virgin olive oil

⅓ cup minced red onion

2 garlic cloves, minced

¾ cup dry white wine

½ cup packaged organic chicken stock

⅓ cup pine nuts, toasted (page 142)

1 cup Easy Peasy Pesto Sauce (page 163)

Salt and freshly ground black pepper

6 red teardrop or cherry tomatoes, halved

Freshly grated Parmesan cheese, for serving

1. Bring a large saucepan of lightly salted water to a boil over high heat. Add the potatoes and cook until barely tender, about 8 minutes. Use a wire sieve or slotted spoon to transfer the potatoes to a colander. Rinse with cold water, drain again, and transfer to a bowl.

2. Add the asparagus to boiling water and cook until crisp-tender, about 4 minutes. Use tongs to transfer the asparagus to a bowl of ice-cold water.

3. Add the green beans to boiling water and cook until crisp-tender, about 4 minutes. Drain in a colander, and rinse under cold water. Pour the asparagus into the colander to drain.

4. Meanwhile, bring a new pot of salted water to a boil over high heat. Add the spaghetti and cook according to the package directions until al dente.

5. As soon the pot goes on to boil, start the sauce. Heat the oil in a large skillet over medium-high heat. Add the onions and garlic and reduce the heat to medium. Cook, stirring occasionally, until the onion is translucent, about 4 minutes. Move the onion mixture to one side of the pan. Add the potatoes to the empty side and cook until lightly browned. Add the asparagus and green beans and cook, stirring often, until heated through, about 2 minutes.

6. Add the wine and bring to a boil over high heat. Simmer until the wine has reduced to a few tablespoons, about 5 minutes. Add the stock and simmer for 5 minutes. Add the pine nuts.

7. Drain the spaghetti and return to the cooking pot. Add the vegetable mixture and the pesto. Toss to coat. Season with salt and pepper. Serve in bowls and top with the tomato halves. Serve hot, with the Parmesan passed on the side.

162

Easy Peasy Pesto Sauce   Makes 3½ cups

IF YOU'RE IN a pinch for time or feeling extra lazy, there are plenty of wonderful pre-packaged pesto sauces. However it's really quite an easy sauce to make, it fills the kitchen with lovely smells, and tastes so delicious fresh! Give it a try, and I promise you won't go back to jars.

2 packed cups basil leaves

1 cup freshly grated Parmesan cheese

½ cup pine nuts, toasted (page 142)

3 garlic cloves

1 cup extra-virgin olive oil, plus more as needed

Salt and freshly ground black pepper

1. Fit a food processor with the metal chopping blade. Add the basil, Parmesan, pine nuts, and garlic and process until ground into a thick paste. With the machine running, gradually add the olive oil until absorbed into the basil mixture. Season with salt and pepper.

Note: If storing, transfer to an airtight container. Pour enough oil over the top of the pesto to cover. Refrigerate for up to 1 month. Before using again, bring to room temperature and stir.

163

Brandied Fruit Coulis   Makes 8 servings

I JUST ADORE homemade fruit sauce poured over fresh ice cream or a slice of cake. And it's such a forgiving recipe: You can use almost any fruit you have on hand—fresh, just past fresh, or canned—in any combination that suits you. Place a ladyfinger or digestive biscuit—you call them cookies in America, I call them delicious no matter where I am—in a bowl, top with ice cream, and ladle the warm fruit coulis over the top. Divine!

165

One 20-ounce can pineapple chunks in pineapple juice

One 12-ounce can peaches in juice

3 cups sliced fresh strawberries, divided

1 cup fresh blueberries

¼ cup orange juice

¼ cup sugar

2 tablespoons fresh lemon juice

¼ cup peach-flavored brandy

Ladyfingers or digestive biscuits

Crème Fraîche (page 68) or vanilla ice cream, for serving

1. Drain the pineapple and peaches, reserving the juices. Cut the peaches into bite-sized chunks. Transfer the pineapple and peaches to a bowl and set aside.

2. Combine the reserved fruit juices, 2 cups water, 1½ cups of sliced strawberries, blueberries, orange juice, sugar, and lemon juice in a medium nonreactive saucepan. Bring to a simmer over medium heat, stirring to dissolve the sugar. Reduce the heat to medium-low and simmer until the blueberries are tender, about 10 minutes.

3. Stir in the brandy, pineapple, peaches, and the remaining 1½ cups strawberries. Serve warm over ladyfingers or digestive biscuits with crème fraîche or ice cream.

Mint Gin and Tonic Makes 1 serving

THERE IS NOTHING easier than a gin and tonic (except perhaps a vodka and tonic, which I also adore—simply substitute vodka for the gin), and nothing more refreshing. You must use truly bitter tonic water (stay away from the fizzy soda—the best brands are sold in single-serving-sized bottles), and serve in a nice, cold glass.

2 ounces London dry gin

½ fresh lime

6 mint leaves

Tonic water

1. Fill an 8-ounce highball glass with ice cubes. Add gin. Squeeze lime juice into glass. Add 4 mint leaves. Stir carefully.

2. Fill glass with tonic water. Add 2 mint leaves to top.

NO-MORE-MALARIA COCKTAIL

The gin and tonic has a fascinating history. It was invented in the eighteenth century as a means to get the British living in India to drink tonic water. Europeans were especially susceptible to malaria when they arrived in Asia, and back then tonic water had large amounts of quinine in it—good for fighting malaria, bad for the taste buds. To counteract the bitterness of the tonic water, the Brits added gin. No one complained further.

166

CHAPTER

{ 9 }

Darling Days

here's nothing more precious than creating a special occasion for or about children. I have thrown the most elegant baby showers, birthday parties, and even play dates that were both kid- and wallet-friendly.

I recently threw a shower for a dear friend of mine who was expecting twins: a boy and a girl. I gave her a pink-and-blue themed tea party. It was very little work, but very pretty. We had finger sandwiches, Champagne, and English tea, of course. Everyone got to take a teacup home as their guest gift, filled with a small bag of chocolates. I adore teacups—almost as much as I love shoes! I am always on the lookout for beautiful cups and saucers, especially at flea markets and vintage shops, because they make such lovely gifts. They needn't match; in fact, I like it better when they don't. Comparing teacups and their different patterns and designs becomes a conversation starter for your guests.

Another baby shower I hosted was called "An Afternoon to Remember." Aside from covering the tables with baby blanket fur, the highlight was the music. I downloaded fifteen of my friend's favorite classic songs—by Ella Fitzgerald, Harry Connick, Jr., and the like—and we had them playing throughout the party. The CD made a lovely present for her to remember the event.

Generally, gatherings to celebrate little ones include presents. Of everything you do, make sure the gift table is done up beautifully as it will be one of the first things people see and the centerpiece of the party. Cover it with cut fabric that matches your theme, and decorate with teddy bears and books interspersed with little vases of flowers. I do believe you

TWO BITES

In any shape, the tea sandwich should ideally be two bites. A whole day's calories for some *Housewives* I know . . .

should allot time for the presents to be opened in front of everyone. A lot of the pleasure people get when giving gifts comes from seeing the recipient's face when she opens it. Don't deny them that.

The key to Darling Days is to make everything in miniature: tiny tasters, mini desserts, and, of course, finger sandwiches. There are any number of combinations of tea sandwiches you can make, but here are my favorites.

TEA SANDWICHES

Before I give you my filling recipes, let's talk about how to properly assemble a tea sandwich. Even the most delicious sandwich will be passed over if it doesn't look divine. There are no rules for the contents: you may spread almost anything inside a tea sandwich, sweet or savory (except maybe peanut butter and jelly, or if you do, I'm not eating them!); you can mix and match fillings with whatever type of bread you prefer; and you can and should be as creative as possible when arranging them. The sky's the limit. Really push yourself to try something new. It's certainly small and inexpensive enough that you needn't fear a costly mistake, and you just might discover you have a petite gift!

- - - - - - - TYPES OF TEA SANDWICHES -

As I mentioned, you can really put anything you'd like inside a tea sandwich: a single layer of jam, flavored cream cheese, cold meat, roasted vegetables, or a creamy salad. You can be as simple as you'd like, or elegant: sliced cucumbers to caviar, anything's allowed!

For me, the bigger decision is how I'm going to present each sandwich. You can cut small squares or simple shapes with a knife, use a cookie cutter to punch out anything from a circle to a flower, or serve them open-faced. No matter which cut you use, here are my top tea sandwich tips:

- **Use frozen bread.** It cuts nicely, and won't scrunch up when you add the spread. Don't worry; it will defrost naturally in less than 30 minutes.
- **If you are cutting shapes by hand with a knife, first remove the crusts from the bread, then assemble your sandwich on whole pieces of bread.** Top it with a second slice before you cut into smaller sizes. This will give you a clean, matched edge on all sides.
- **If you can, ask your baker to slice a whole loaf in horizontal rather than vertical slices for you.** You'll get more surface area and less waste that way. Slices $\frac{1}{4}$ inch thick are ideal.
- **Don't toss the extra bread scraps!** You can freeze them for future bread crumbs or stuffings, to plump up a meatloaf, or to create a delicious bread pudding.
- **To keep sandwiches you've made ahead of time from drying out, cover them loosely with waxed paper,** then gently lay a damp kitchen towel over them before sticking them in the refrigerator.

You can be as simple as you like, or elegant ... —*Lisa Vanderpump*

- - - - - - - DARLING SANDWICH IDEAS -

Vary the Shapes

I think small rectangles look rather nice all lined up on a pretty platter, but I wouldn't want all my sandwiches to look the same. Triangles are always elegant. You can use flower shapes, then cut a smaller flower window in the top bread to show a peek of the filling below—very pretty. I've also used a solid bottom and crossed two thin strips on top to make a little "X" kiss shape.

Vary the Bread

Using all white bread is far too boring. I like to use different flavored and different colored breads as well. Or mix them up on the same sandwich. You can get a nice effect using a darker color bread on the bottom and a lighter on top, especially if you lay them out like a checkerboard.

Choose a bread with a "tight crumb," that is, one that doesn't have big holes. If you use a bread that is too holey, the filling will fall out of the sandwich.

Your baker can also dye bread for you. I had some bread made pale blue for a baby boy shower—not all the bread, just mixed in here and there for fantastic visual impact.

Edge Your Sandwiches

Rolling at least one of your sandwich shapes in a chopped color or texture will add to the entire presentation. Spread a thin layer of plain yogurt around the edges, then roll the sandwich in chopped nuts, poppy seeds, or finely diced parsley.

Garnish Your Sandwiches

Top a few sandwiches with a toothpick speared with a bright red grape tomato or olive. Fresh greens and herbs like parsley or rosemary also look lovely sitting on top.

Open-Faced Art

If you've got the time and want to get really creative, I urge you to try decorating some open-faced sandwiches. Start with an even layer of cream cheese on the bottom slice. (Use plain white for some, and colored for others.) Then cut vegetables or fruits into paper-thin slices. Use a small knife to pare them down even more. Cucumbers make lovely strips. Layer the slices on a slight overlap. Place seeds or spices in decorative rows around them.

It can be as simple as just edging the sandwich—or you might unleash your inner Picasso and make diagonals, ocean waves, even initials. Fresh green herb leaves can be flattened and pressed onto the sandwiches in different patterns: try flat Italian parsley, mint leaves, fresh dill, tarragon, chives that can be bent into really nice shapes—really anything edible that is pleasing to the eye. Strawberries, thin slices of red pepper, or red caviar can add another dimension of color. And nothing beats edible flowers: pansies, snapdragons, violas or orchids. Just make sure they are pesticide free and meant for eating!

Pinky's Homemade
Strawberry Cream Cheese

OF COURSE I HAD to give you my own recipe for strawberry cream cheese since it's pink and tastes far better than anything you could buy in the store.

One 8-ounce package
cream cheese, softened

1 tablespoon confectioners' sugar

1 cup fresh strawberries, hulled

Mix all ingredients in a blender or food processor until smooth. You can also substitute 4 tablespoons of strawberry jam for the fresh strawberries and sugar.

CHILD-FRIENDLY TEA SANDWICHES

Even on Darling Days, I find that the guests celebrating children are usually adults, but you might want to have some child-friendly sandwich offerings as well. Anything in a recognizable shape or given a fun name is sure to be embraced by a child. In Britain, we make it a habit of cutting our regular children's sandwiches into 1-inch-thick strips, rather than just cutting them diagonally. We christen the strips "soldiers," and the children gobble them up. You might also try matching the shape of the sandwich to the filling inside. For instance, an apple shaped sandwich might have a fruit filling. And nothing is cuter than tuna fish sandwiches cut like little fishies.

176

Prosciutto Tea Sandwiches with Fig Butter

Makes about 20 tea sandwiches

I LOVE THIS flavor combination: the wonderfully salty smoked prosciutto with the sweet fig and Russian black bread.

4 tablespoons unsalted butter, softened

20 slices Russian black bread, crusts trimmed

4 tablespoons fig preserves

10 thin slices prosciutto

3 cups baby spinach

1. Butter 10 bread slices. Spread with a thin layer of the preserves. Divide the prosciutto and spinach evenly over the slices.

2. Butter the remaining bread slices. Place, buttered sides down, on the prepared slices to make sandwiches. Cut as desired.

3. Transfer to a platter, cover loosely, and refrigerate until ready to serve, up to 4 hours.

------- VARIATION -------------------------------

Open-Faced Alternative

You could also serve this as an open-faced sandwich. Spread butter and fig preserves on bottom slice of bread. Layer prosciutto evenly in one thin slice. Trim to shape with a sharp knife. Garnish with baby spinach, an asparagus tip, or a rosette of very thinly sliced melon held on with a dollop of plain cream cheese.

177

Chicken Salad Tea Sandwiches with Toasted Almonds

Makes about 3 cups salad, 20 tea sandwiches

⅔ cup (about 3 ounces) natural sliced almonds

½ cup mayonnaise

2 medium celery ribs, finely chopped

½ cup seeded and finely chopped green pepper

¼ cup finely chopped yellow onion

1 teaspoon Hungarian sweet paprika

2 cups finely chopped cooked chicken

Salt and freshly ground black pepper

20 slices sourdough bread, crusts trimmed

1. Preheat the oven to 350°F. Spread the almonds on a baking sheet. Bake, stirring occasionally, until lightly browned, about 8 minutes. Let cool. Finely chop the almonds. Spread the almonds on a plate.

2. Mix the mayonnaise, celery, green pepper, onion, and paprika in a medium bowl. Add the chicken and mix again. Season with salt and pepper. Cover and refrigerate for at least 2 hours, or preferably overnight.

3. Using a cookie cutter about 2½ inches in diameter, cut out 40 decorative shapes from the sliced bread. Spread about 2½ tablespoons of the chicken filling on 20 of the bread slices, and top with the remaining slices. Press the top of each sandwich slightly so the salad peeks out from the sides. Roll the edges of each sandwich in the almonds. Transfer to a platter, cover loosely, and refrigerate until ready to serve, up to 4 hours.

Smoked Salmon Tea Sandwiches

Makes about 12 tea sandwiches

½ cup mayonnaise

1 tablespoon finely chopped fresh dill

1 tablespoon finely chopped shallot

1 tablespoon drained and rinsed nonpareil capers

2 teaspoons prepared horseradish

Salt and freshly ground black pepper

2 tablespoons unsalted butter, at room temperature

12 slices pumpernickel bread, crusts trimmed

6 wide, thin slices smoked salmon

1. Mix the mayonnaise with dill, shallot, capers, and horseradish in a small bowl. Season with salt and pepper.

2. Butter half of the bread slices. Top with the mayonnaise mixture and the salmon. Butter the remaining bread slices. Place, buttered sides down, on the prepared slices to make sandwiches. Cut as desired.

3. Transfer to a platter, cover loosely, and refrigerate until ready to serve, up to 4 hours.

Dilled Egg Salad Tea Sandwiches

Makes 2 cups egg salad, 16 tea sandwiches

YES, I AM GIVING you instructions on how to hard-boil an egg. Don't take offense; I'm sure you're naturally great at it. But for a perfect egg salad, we need perfectly cooked eggs. Green-ringed yolks would never do!

6 large eggs

⅓ cup mayonnaise

1 medium celery rib, finely diced

1 tablespoon finely chopped fresh dill, plus 16 small dill sprigs for garnish

1 tablespoon finely chopped shallot

1 teaspoon Dijon mustard

Salt and freshly ground black pepper

16 slices white bread, crusts trimmed

1. Place the eggs in a medium saucepan and add enough cold water to cover. Bring to a boil over medium-high heat. Remove from the heat and cover the saucepan. Let stand for 15 minutes. Using a slotted spoon, transfer the eggs to a bowl of ice water. Let cool. Crack and peel the eggs under a thin stream of cold running water. Chop the eggs.

2. Mix the mayonnaise, celery, chopped dill, shallot, and mustard together in a medium bowl. Add the eggs, mix again, and season with salt and pepper. Cover and refrigerate at least 2 hours, or preferably overnight.

3. Using a cookie cutter about 2½ inches in diameter, cut 32 decorative shapes from the sliced bread. Spread each with about 2 tablespoons of egg salad, and top with the remaining slices. Transfer to a platter, cover loosely, and refrigerate until ready to serve, up to 4 hours. Just before serving, top each sandwich with a dill sprig.

A darling day would not be complete without platters of tiny cookies and pastries for dessert. You can purchase gorgeous cookie trays with great variation at any grocery, but here are a couple of uniquely British desserts that you can make yourself.

Shortbread Cups with Chocolate Cream Makes 3 dozen

THESE ARE PRETTY as a picture, and not difficult to make—if you have nonstick mini-muffin pans and a little wooden gadget called a tart tamper to help shape the dough into cups. You can find the tamper at kitchenware shops or online.

183

Shortbread Crust	Filling
1½ cups all-purpose flour	1 tablespoon plus 1½ teaspoons all-purpose flour
2 tablespoons white rice flour or cornstarch	1 tablespoon plus 1½ teaspoons unsweetened cocoa powder, preferably Dutch processed
⅛ teaspoon salt	¾ cup heavy cream
1 cup (2 sticks) unsalted butter	12 tablespoons (1½ sticks) unsalted butter, at room temperature
½ cup confectioners' sugar	½ cup confectioners' sugar, plus more for garnish
1 teaspoon vanilla extract	½ teaspoon vanilla extract
	36 fresh raspberries

1. To make the crust, sift the flour, rice flour, and salt together into a bowl. Beat the butter and confectioners' sugar together in a medium bowl with an electric mixer on high speed until light in color and texture, about 2 minutes. Beat in the vanilla. Gradually stir in the flour mixture. Gather the dough up into a thick disk, wrap in plastic wrap, and refrigerate until chilled, about 2 hours.

2. Position racks in the center and top third of the oven and preheat the oven to 350°F. Spray 3 mini-muffin pans (preferably nonstick) with nonstick spray. Roll the dough into 36 equal balls. Press each ball of dough into the bottom and sides of a mini-muffin cup. (If you have a wooden tart tamper, use it to press the dough into the cups.) Pierce the dough with a fork and freeze for 15 minutes.

3. Bake for 10 minutes. Remove the pans from the oven and quickly pierce with a fork to deflate the puffed cups. Return to the oven and continue baking until the cups are golden brown, about 10 minutes longer. If the pans are nonstick, the baking time may be a little shorter because the dark pans absorb the oven heat and bake the crusts more quickly than shiny pans. Let cool in the pans for 5 minutes. Carefully remove the cups from the pans, transfer to a wire cake rack, and let cool completely.

4. To make the filling, whisk the flour and cocoa together in a small saucepan. Whisk in a few tablespoons of the cream to dissolve the flour and cocoa and make a paste, then whisk in the remaining cream. Whisk over medium-low heat until thick and boiling. Transfer to a small bowl, press plastic wrap directly on the cocoa mixture surface to keep a skin from forming, and cool completely.

5. Beat the butter, ½ cup confectioners' sugar, and vanilla together in a medium bowl with an electric mixer on low speed until combined. Increase the speed to high, beat in the cooled cocoa mixture, and beat until light and fluffy, about 1 minute.

6. Transfer the cocoa filling to a pastry bag fitted with a ½-inch-wide fluted pastry tip. Pipe the filling into the cups. (Or, simply spoon the filling into a 1-gallon plastic food storage bag, snip off one corner of the bag about ½ inch from the point, and use as an impromptu pastry bag. It isn't as decorative, but it works.) Top each with a raspberry, sift confectioners' sugar on top, and serve.

MALTESERS SUNDAES

ICE CREAM BRINGS out the darling in everyone, doesn't it? Especially sundaes. In Britain, Maltesers are chocolate-covered malted milk balls with a honeycombed center. What makes these special is how I present them. Serve scoops of rich vanilla ice cream in tall sundae glasses. Then spoon homemade hot fudge sauce at the table for your guests. Finally, pass around several silver trays with little teaspoons and bowls of toppings: mini candies, crushed pretzels, chopped nuts, fresh fruit, Whipped Cream (page 68), and of course whole and crushed malted milk balls!

Homemade Hot Fudge Sauce   Makes about 2 cups

STORE-BOUGHT SAUCE just doesn't compare to homemade hot fudge sauce— come to think of it, I might consider this a pantry staple! And it's so easy to make! This recipe is almost impossible to mess up, as you don't have to melt any sugar and risk burning it, or even use a double boiler.

One 14-ounce can sweetened condensed milk

½ cup (3 ounces) high-quality semisweet chocolate chips

4 tablespoons (¼ cup) unsalted butter, cut into small cubes

½ teaspoon vanilla extract

1. Combine the condensed milk, chocolate chips, and butter in a heavy-bottomed, medium saucepan. Cook over medium heat, stirring constantly, until the chocolate is melted. Remove from the heat. Stir in the vanilla. Serve warm.

DRINKS

Raspberry Pomegranate Lemonade   Makes 8 servings

1 cup sugar

³/₄ cup fresh or
thawed frozen raspberries

1 cup pomegranate juice

1 cup fresh lemon juice
(from about 8 lemons)

1. Bring the sugar and 1 cup of water to a boil in a small sauce-pan, stirring until the sugar dissolves to create simple syrup. Remove from the heat and let cool completely.

2. Purée the raspberries in food processor or blender. Strain through a fine mesh sieve to remove the seeds.

3. Mix the raspberry purée, cooled simple syrup, pomegranate juice, and lemon juice in large pitcher. Add 6 to 9 cups cold water depending on how strong you like your lemonade. Serve over ice.

Hot Mint Tea   Makes 3 to 4 servings

HOT MINT TEA is very popular in Morocco, which in turn is a popular destination spot for Brits (and New York *Housewives* apparently). I highly encourage you to grow your own mint. It does well outdoors even after a harsh winter, but can also thrive inside on a sunny window sill. And it's great to have on hand for both cooking and garnishing.

⅓ cup firmly packed fresh mint leaves, plus extra leaves for garnish

1 bag green tea

⅓ cup sugar

2 tablespoons fresh lemon juice

1. Wash the mint leaves. Bring 1⅓ cups of water to a boil in a large saucepan. Add the tea bag and sugar. Remove from heat and stir well. Cover and let steep for 1 hour. Remove and discard tea bag.

2. Add lemon juice and 1⅓ cups water. Return to a boil. Remove from heat. Serve hot. (Leftovers can be cooled and served over ice as a wonderful iced tea.)

187

THE MORE THINGS CHANGE . . .

When I am cooking, my children are like bees to a honey pot, trying to scrounge a piece here or taste something there. With my spoon at the ready, I threaten to swat their precious hands as soon as they venture near. Now that they are older, they still hover, but with the intention of not just eating but taking all the leftovers. I am constantly replenishing the Tupperware in my cupboard!

CHAPTER

{ 10 }

Chubby Days

ALWAYS LAUGH WHEN I see "skinny" this and "skinny" that. You can't be on a diet all the time! And why should you be? I absolutely hate this national obsession with looking like a toothpick. There's nothing natural about it. Or sexy for that matter. Just ask most men: Would you rather shag a bony thing that seems as if it might break or do you prefer luscious curves? I promise you I know the answer. Skinny is not all it's cut out to be.

Shall I starve myself to look so thin that I haven't the energy to enjoy my life? And then drug myself just to be able to get out of bed? I can't say that sounds like much of a life to me.

Having owned restaurants for so many years, I have a deep appreciation for food. I'm not sure I could shake it if I tried. And I don't know too many skinny chefs—nor would I want to eat at their establishments! Perhaps my round bottom is to thank for my culinary success!

And so I present to you: Chubby Days. Decadent dishes for those days when you just don't give a damn.

Now, before the nutritionists of the world get their knickers in a twist, I am not suggesting you eat like this all day every day. To do so would be just as bad for your body as starving yourself. It's that balance we must find. I am a huge advocate of healthy eating. I don't put processed or fast food junk into my body. And I make no secret of the fact that it is much harder to maintain your weight the older you get. I could enjoy far more Chubby Days when I was younger. But as long as you are sensible about eating, get enough exercise—at least half an hour of something vigorous five times a week—and minimize your carb intake at night, you will be fine!

So that being said . . . pass me another cookie.

Bangers & Mash

Makes 6 servings

IT DOES SOUND rather naughty, and can look a bit naughty when you're eating it, I'll admit, but bangers & mash is simply a mildly seasoned sausage served with mashed potatoes. But I urge you to find a proper Cumberland sausage. There's nothing like it in the world.

2 tablespoons olive oil, divided

12 link pork sausages, mild
(about 1 ½ pounds total),
each pierced once with a fork

2 shallots, sliced

1 garlic clove, minced

3 tablespoons all-purpose flour

3 cups apple cider

Mashed Potatoes (page 58)

1. Position a rack in the center of the oven and preheat to 350°F.

2. Heat 1 tablespoon of the oil in a large, ovenproof skillet over medium-high heat. Add the sausage and cook, turning occasionally, until browned, about 5 minutes. Transfer the sausages to a plate.

3. Add the remaining 1 tablespoon oil and the shallots to the skillet. Reduce the heat to medium-low. Cook, stirring often, until the shallots soften, about 2 minutes. Add the garlic and cook until it is fragrant, about 30 seconds. Sprinkle in the flour and stir well. Stir in the cider and bring to a simmer. Return the sausages to the skillet and cover.

4. Bake for 20 minutes. Uncover and bake until the gravy thickens and the sausages are cooked through, about 5 minutes.

5. To serve, spoon the mashed potatoes onto plates. Add the sausages and top with gravy.

BANG, BANG

We call sausages "bangers" in the U.K. because in the past, when the skin shrunk as you cooked them, they did explode on occasion. It was quite common during World War II because extra water was added to sausages due to meat being rationed.

Spotted Dick Makes 6 to 8 servings

FROM BANGERS TO DICK, you're starting to think you bought a different kind of book, aren't you? Spotted dick is in fact a traditional English steamed pudding (where the pudding is steamed in a special mold called a "pudding pot" over simmering water on the stove) with dried fruit. The dried fruit bits are the "spots," but I can't vouch for how the word "dick" got associated with a pudding. Some food historians believe it was a muddling of accents from "pudding" to "puddick." Others say that "dick" was a name for cheese in the 1800s. In any case, I think you'll agree it is quite delicious. Pudding pots for steaming aren't found as readily in stores here in the States as they are in Britain, but you don't need one for my recipe, as I like to bake mine as a roll. Turn to the next page to see how exquisite the finished dish can look.

193

Filling	Dough
Unsalted butter or vegetable shortening, for the foil	1½ cups all-purpose flour, plus more for rolling out dough
½ cup seedless raisins	1 tablespoon sugar
⅓ cup packed light brown sugar	1½ teaspoons baking powder
¼ cup dried currants	¼ teaspoon salt
¼ cup chopped dates	8 tablespoons chilled vegetable shortening, cut into ½-inch pieces
Grated zest of 1 lemon	½ cup whole milk
1 teaspoon apple pie spice or ¼ teaspoon each ground cinnamon, ground cloves, ground allspice, and freshly grated nutmeg	**Custard Sauce**
	2 cups whole milk
	6 large egg yolks
	½ cup sugar
	¾ teaspoon vanilla extract

1. Position a rack in the center of the oven and preheat to 350°F. Tear off an 18-inch-long sheet of aluminum foil, and butter the foil.

2. To make the filling, combine the raisins, brown sugar, currants, dates, lemon zest, and spices in a small bowl.

3. To make the dough, sift the flour, sugar, baking powder, and salt together into a medium bowl. Add the shortening. Using a pastry blender or two knives, cut in the shortening until the mixture resembles coarse crumbs with some pea-sized pieces. Stir in the milk to make a soft dough. Gather up the dough in the bowl.

4. Place the dough on well-floured work surface and dust the top with flour. Roll out into an 8 × 12-inch rectangle, with the long side facing you. Spread the dried fruit filling over the dough, leaving a ½-inch border of dough at the top. Brush the exposed dough with cold water. Starting at the long end near you, roll up the dough and press the long seam closed. Place the foil next to you, buttered side up. Using a long metal spatula as an aide, transfer the roll to the center of the foil. Bring up the foil to loosely enclose the roll (it should not be tightly wrapped), and crimp the packet closed. Transfer to a baking sheet.

5. Bake until the roll has risen and lightly browned (carefully open the foil to check), about 1 hour.

6. Meanwhile, make the custard sauce. Place a bowl with a wire sieve near the stove. Heat the milk in a heavy-bottomed, medium saucepan over medium heat until small bubbles appear around the edges. Remove from the heat. Whisk the egg yolks and sugar together in a heatproof bowl until pale and thick, about 1 minute. Gradually whisk in the hot milk, then return to the saucepan. Cook over medium-low heat, stirring constantly with a wooden spoon (and being sure to get into the corners of the saucepan), until the custard reads 185°F on an instant-read thermometer and is thick enough to lightly coat the spoon. (If you run your finger through the custard on the spoon, it will cut a swath.) Immediately strain the custard through the sieve into the bowl. Stir in the vanilla. The sauce can be served warm or chilled. To chill quickly, place the bowl in a larger bowl of icy water, and stir often.

7. Unwrap the roll (watch out for steam), and cut crosswise into thick slices. Transfer each slice to a bowl, add the custard sauce, and serve warm.

QUICK CUSTARD

If you're crunched for time, and if your market carries it—look in the international or British section—you can whip up a quick custard using a packet of Bird's Custard Sauce. Or, if it's the holiday season, store-bought eggnog makes a lovely substitute.

Millionaire's Shortbread   Makes 24 bar cookies

AS IF BUTTERY shortbread wasn't delicious enough, in Britain we've gone and topped it with *dulce de leche* and chocolate. It's almost as rich as Andy Cohen. Almost.

12 tablespoons (1½ sticks) unsalted butter, at room temperature, plus more for the baking pan

¼ cup sugar

1½ cups all-purpose flour, plus more for the baking pan

Pinch of salt

One 14-ounce can dulce de leche, warmed until spreadable

10 ½ ounces (three 3.5-ounce bars) semisweet or bittersweet chocolate, finely chopped

1 ½ teaspoons vegetable shortening

1. Position a rack in the center of the oven and preheat to 350°F. Lightly butter a 9-inch-square baking pan. Line the bottom and 2 sides of the pan with an 18-inch-long strip of aluminum foil, letting the excess foil hang over the sides. Lightly butter the foil. Dust the inside of the pan with flour and tap out the excess flour.

2. Beat the butter and sugar together in a medium bowl with an electric mixer on high speed until light in color and texture, about 3 minutes. With the mixer on low speed, add the flour and salt and mix until the dough clumps together. Press firmly and evenly into the prepared pan. Pierce the dough all over with a fork. Bake until the shortbread is lightly browned, about 25 minutes. Cool in the pan on a wire rack for 20 minutes. Freeze until chilled, about 30 minutes.

3. Spread the dulce de leche over the shortbread. Freeze until the dulce de leche is set and chilled, about 20 minutes.

4. Melt the chocolate and shortening together in the top part of a double boiler set over very hot, but not simmering, water, stirring occasionally. Pour the melted chocolate over the dulce de leche, smoothing with a metal spatula. Let the chocolate layer set at room temperature.

5. Lift up on the foil "handles" to remove the pastry from the pan in one piece. Using a sharp, thin-bladed knife, cut into 24 equal bars.

DULCE DE LECHE

I won't have you making anything from scratch that takes a terribly long time or is overly complicated, and dulce de leche is one of those things. Look for jars of it at specialty food stores like William-Sonoma or in the Latino food aisle of many supermarkets.

English Sticky Toffee Pudding

Makes 9 servings

THIS IS ONE of the desserts Villa Blanca is famous for. Even though it's called a "pudding" it's not the creamy American dessert—it's really a cake with a warm toffee sauce. And it tastes like melted heaven on a plate.

Cake

¾ cup pitted and chopped dates

1 teaspoon baking soda

1 cup plus 1 tablespoon all-purpose flour, plus flour for the baking dish

1 teaspoon baking powder

¼ teaspoon salt

4 tablespoons (½ stick) unsalted butter, at room temperature, plus more for the baking dish

¾ cup sugar

1 large egg, lightly beaten

1 teaspoon vanilla extract

Toffee Sauce

1 cup packed light brown sugar

8 tablespoons (1 stick) unsalted butter, cut into tablespoons

½ cup heavy cream

Whipped Cream (page 68)

1. To make the cake, combine the dates and baking soda in a small bowl with 1 cup boiling water. Let cool, about 1 hour. (The baking soda soak softens the tough date skin; don't skip this step.)

2. Position a rack in the center of the oven and preheat to 350°F. Butter and flour a 9-inch-square metal baking dish.

3. Sift the flour, baking powder, and salt together. Beat the butter and sugar together in a medium bowl with an electric mixer on high speed until light in color and texture, about 3 minutes. Beat in the egg and vanilla. Reduce the mixer speed to low. Gradually add the flour mixture and beat until combined. Add the cooled dates with their soaking liquid and fold together until the batter is smooth. Scrape into the baking dish and smooth the top.

4. Bake until the cake springs back when pressed in the center, about 35 minutes.

5. Meanwhile, make the toffee sauce. Bring the brown sugar, butter, and cream to a boil in a heavy medium saucepan over medium-high heat, stirring often to dissolve the sugar. Reduce the heat to medium and cook at a brisk boil, stirring often, until lightly thickened, about 8 minutes. Remove from the heat. The sauce will cool but remain warm from the saucepan's residual heat.

6. Remove the cake from the oven. Position the broiler rack about 6 inches from the source of heat and preheat on high. Spread ½ cup of the toffee sauce over the top of the cake. Broil until bubbling, about 30 seconds. Remove from the broiler and let stand for 5 minutes.

7. To serve, cut the cake into 9 equal pieces and transfer each piece to a bowl. Top each with a portion of the remaining toffee sauce and a spoonful of whipped cream. Serve warm.

MARTINIS

I'm not even going to tell you why I've listed martinis in this chapter. It's better you don't know, or you'll never enjoy one again. But since we are celebrating the good life, I assure you, there's no better way.

White Chocolate Martini   Makes 1 serving

For a really spectacular visual effect (although you can serve this ungarnished and be equally satisfied), swirl circles of chocolate syrup into the glass before you pour in the martini. Garnish with a dark chocolate rod.

1½ ounces vodka
1 ounce white chocolate liqueur
1½ ounces heavy cream

1. Fill a cocktail shaker halfway with ice cubes. Add the vodka and shake vigorously 10 times.

2. Add the white chocolate liqueur and cream. Shake 10 more times. Strain into a chilled martini glass.

PROPER MEASURING

At a bar, you may see the bartender "free pour" cocktail ingredients without measuring, but that kind of precision comes with much practice. At home, to be sure that you get the same delectable results every time, use a jigger. This measuring tool, which looks like two differently sized cones attached at their bottoms, comes in a variety of size combinations, but the 1 ounce-1 ½ ounce combination is the most useful for most single-drink recipes.

IT'S BECOME QUITE fashionable to rim martini glasses with sugar or even bits of candy. If you'd like, rub a cut strawberry around the rim of your glass to moisten it, then dip in a small plate of rimming sugar—pink sugar will look lovely.

Strawberry Martini Makes 1 serving

2 large fresh strawberries

2 ounces vodka

1 teaspoon crème de cassis or black currant liqueur

1 teaspoon fresh lime juice

1 teaspoon sugar, preferably superfine or bartenders' sugar

1. Muddle 1 strawberry in the bottom of a cocktail shaker with a muddler or wooden spoon. Add 2 or 3 ice cubes. Add vodka, crème de cassis, lime juice, and sugar. Shake for 10 seconds. Strain into a chilled martini glass.

2. Cut remaining strawberry at the tip and set on the edge of the glass.

201

MODERN MUDDLERS

If you often crush fresh fruit for drinks or desserts, a muddler is a wonderful addition to your kitchen tool drawer. Traditional muddlers are rounded wooden sticks (I understand Jamie Oliver uses the end of a rolling pin as his muddler, but try as I might, I can't seem to get mine to fit into a glass, though a wooden spoon does work well . . .) but modern muddlers are much, much better. Made of steel and grippable rubber, they have jagged little teeth on the bottom that help rip fruit into juicy pieces rather than just flattening them to death. You can find them at kitchen stores or online for around $15.

Dirty Martini

Makes 1 serving

DO I EVEN have to tell you I like my martinis dirty? Well, sometimes anyway . . .
You can use the olive brine from a jar of olives as your olive flavoring, but then your olives
will shrivel up, won't they? I prefer to buy a bottle of olive juice (which is what the label
says although it is really brine) specifically for making dirty martinis.

¼ ounce dry vermouth

2 ounces gin

1 ounce olive juice

3 pimento-stuffed green olives

1. Pour the vermouth into a chilled martini glass. Swirl to coat the inside of the glass, then pour out the vermouth.

2. Fill a cocktail shaker halfway with ice cubes. Add the gin and olive juice. Shake 4 to 5 times. Strain into a chilled martini glass. Spear the olives onto a cocktail stick and add to the martini.

ICE COLD

Martinis must be served in an ice-cold glass. Pop your glasses and your cocktail shaker in the freezer for at least a half hour before you plan on mixing drinks.

EXTRA PUDDING DROPPER

I didn't want to leave you dirty, and I am quite open about everything, so I'll admit I do have a secret "skinny" recipe of my own. If I've had too many Chubby Days in a row, I use a Chinese-based soup to help me drop some of the extra "pudding" (a lovely nickname we have for "fat" in Britain). It's dreadfully simple and very delicious. It takes only ten minutes to go from start to your table. (Leaving you plenty of time to run to the gym!)

Baby Bok Choy Soup   Makes 1 big serving

TO SAVE TIME, add the food to the saucepan in the order given so one thing cooks while the next ingredient is being prepped. This is just my basic recipe; feel free to add and subtract to your heart's content. A teaspoon of minced fresh ginger and a chopped garlic clove are nice additions, as are sweet corn or sliced water chestnuts. I sometimes use butter-flied shelled shrimp instead of the chicken. A handful of cooked thin noodles or a big spoonful of cooked rice are also good, but don't cook them directly in the broth, or they'll make it cloudy and too thick. Add these towards the end of the cooking time, after you're sure that the chicken is cooked through.

1¾ cups packaged organic chicken stock

1 tablespoon dry white wine

1 teaspoon soy sauce

Pinch of crushed hot red pepper flakes

One 5- to 6-ounce boneless and skinless chicken breast half

1 baby bok choy

1 scallion, trimmed

Salt and freshly ground black pepper

1. Combine the stock, ¾ cup water, wine, and soy sauce in a medium saucepan over medium-high heat.

2. While the broth mixture is heating, cut the chicken against the grain into very thin (less than ⅛-inch-thick) slices. Add to the broth mixture and let it continue heating.

3. Cut the baby bok choy in half lengthwise. Cut out the thick triangular core. Place the halves cut sides down, and cut crosswise into very thin slices. Add to the heating broth.

4. Cut the scallion crosswise into very thin rounds and add to the heating broth. Let come to a full simmer. Season with salt and pepper. Pour into a very large bowl and serve hot.

ACKNOWLEDGMENTS

OH, WHERE DO I START? A huge thank you to Chris Navratil, Craig Herman, Jennifer Kasius, Frances Soo Ping Chow, Jason Varney, Rick Rodgers, and Heather Maclean who were instrumental in helping me create such a beautiful book; to Simon Green at CAA who encouraged me to venture into the unknown; to Pandora, my daughter, for looking over my shoulder and patiently correcting my mistakes; to Rosia who helps me organize my chaotic life; and to the sex monster Giggy for his unconditional affection.

Also many thanks to my fans who I adore communicating with on Twitter, who keep me real, and most of all, keep me laughing.

And lastly, to my husband of 29 years: thank you Darling for allowing me to grow, to mature, to take so many chances, to have confidence, to trust my instinct, and to follow my dreams knowing that if all went awry, I have the security of a man who truly loves me.

INDEX

207

A FOND FAREWELL

I HOPE YOU'VE enjoyed my little book as much as I've enjoyed writing it for you. It gives me great pleasure to serve good food to good people, and I know you'll enjoy these recipes for many years to come.

If you ever find yourself in Beverly Hills, please drop by and say hello at Villa Blanca. You'll find Ken, Giggy, and myself there most days . . . and nights. And we would very much love to see you.

208